Welcome to the Total Coarse Fishing Yearbook, which I hope will inspire you to go out and put a new personal best on the bank, or target new species from different venues.

Anglers have plenty of good things to shout about – angling is still the biggest participation sport in the UK, even though there are some who will claim otherwise, and tell you that it's in decline. We need to put aside any such negatives and embrace the fantastic sport that's on offer, much of it on our own doorsteps.

The rise in popularity of the commercial fishery has in many cases enabled anglers to drive right up to their chosen swims, and they have certainly taken away the drudge of long walks over muddy fields and challenging stiles. But don't just think your local commercial is just a carp-bagging water, as these venues are now providing some of the best stillwater roach and perch catches ever reported in the angling press and online forums.

However, let's not dismiss our rivers just yet. Although many agree that predation is a real issue, the roach and dace shoals are slowly returning. Then there's the chub and barbel fishing – our traditional big-fish rivers are still giving up personal bests and near-record specimens, but they're not easy to catch. Well that's nothing new, and it's all part of the challenge.

This book features a wide range of venues, and tactics from some of Britain's top anglers, including three former match fishing world champions – Bob Nudd on the Warwickshire Avon in search of barbel on the float, Alan Scotthorne with some great tips on Method-feeder fishing and Will Raison catching silver fish on the waggler at top commercial Gold Valley.

Our specialist anglers include Alan Stagg fishing for crucian carp on simple feeder tactics and Ade Kiddell on traditional methods for big bronze bream. And have you ever tried for specimen rudd… from a river? Gareth Goldson is our man in the know there, and he shows you how with just a loaf of bread. How's that for variety?

Nowadays, chub are appearing in many of our stillwaters, which are not seen as their natural home, but try telling them that. Mick Brown has his sights set on some of these monster fish, but he has to find them first. Then there are two completely different barbel features as England matchman Darren Cox shows you that it is possible to catch them on small rivers on the pole, while big-fish angler Adam Tilford reveals his tactics to tackle big, fast-water weir pools.

As for canals, there are miles of untapped fishing – much of it free – that we often totally ignore, but James Robbins knows just how to get the best out of a day on the cut.

The Total Coarse Fishing Yearbook is a feature-filled read that provides all the tips, techniques and tactics you need to spend an enjoyable, rod-bending day on the bank, whatever the water, with top rigs and a little watercraft to aid your fish finding once you're there. I hope you enjoy it.

Tight lines.

Steve Martin
Deputy Editor
Total Coarse Fishing

Contents

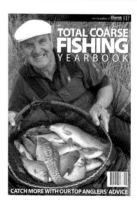

Published by David Hall Publishing Ltd. The advertisements and editorial content of this publication are the copyright of David Hall Publishing Ltd and may not be quoted, copied or reproduced without prior permission of the publisher.

Copyright © 2012

Compiled and edited by **Steve Martin**
Layout and design by **Nicola Howe**
Sub edited by **David Haynes**
Reprographics by **Derek Mooney** and **Adam Mason**

Adam's first bite of the day saw this fabulous 12lb 6oz barbel fall to his feeder-and-boilie setup.

POWER in the POOL!

If you're looking for some rod-wrenching early season river action, Adam Tilford advises you to head for your nearest weir pool.

Nobody would argue that Britain's rivers have changed massively in recent years, and anglers who prefer running water have had to adapt to continue fishing the places they like best.

While the smaller fish in many rivers have become increasingly difficult to catch, big-fish numbers have grown considerably and the chances are you'll now see more carp rods and Baitrunners than you will poles and floats.

There's no better example of this than the Trent. No longer are the banks of this mighty river lined with match anglers every weekend, fishing for the vast shoals of roach and chub that used to abound here. Now, the Trent is a specialist's dream, with carp, chub, bream, pike and even zander now regularly caught to a size to please any big-fish angler.

The changes to the Trent have seen one species above all others hit the headlines. If you want a big barbel in the first few weeks of the season, look no further.

But where do you head to if you want to catch a big 'whiskers'? Well, as far as the Trent is concerned, and any other river for that matter, your prime destination is a weir pool. Now weir pools don't come much bigger than the one at Beeston in Nottingham, and one man who knows this only too well is local angler Adam Tilford.

The 28-year-old joiner has been fishing the Trent since he was 10, witnessing at first hand the gradual increase in the size of barbel and other species in the river. The 30Plus-sponsored angler's barbel fishing exploits were topped earlier this year when he landed a 17lb 6oz monster from the river, and he was only too keen to show us the methods that have made him one of the Trent's leading specialists.

Adam Tilford

Hometown: Nottingham
Sponsor: 30Plus

Fishery Fact File

River Trent, Beeston Weir, Nottingham NG9 1NG

Day tickets: Free fishing, rod licence required

Parking: Street parking nearby

Adam's Top Five Tips For Cracking Weir Pools

1 They fish best when river levels are a bit higher than normal.

2 Arrive before daylight, or fish through the night if allowed. The last two hours of darkness are often best.

3 Summer is the best time to fish weir pools, when much of the river is slow and sluggish.

4 Have at least two rods set up, or more if you have them, so you can cast to different areas.

5 If you're fishing at night in an urban area, don't fish alone. Make sure there are at least two of you on the bank.

Best Baits

Large halibut pellets and yellow boilies are Adam's favourite hook baits for a weir-pool 'lunker'.

Daunting Prospect

"I've fished this river for years and, although I don't catch the numbers of fish that I used to, the fish that I do catch are getting bigger and bigger," he said. "Now I tend to target the barbel but I don't care what I catch, as when the rod tip goes the chances are it will be a big fish."

Big fish can now be caught from anywhere on the river, but for early season reliability, the extra oxygen that weir pools provide mean they are a magnet for fish like barbel. Other species such as bream and chub will also prefer to live here.

Tackling a large weir pool like the one at Beeston can be a daunting prospect, but Adam had a few pointers for anyone fishing one for the first time.

"Basically, you catch from anywhere within a weir pool but there are some areas that you should target more than others," he said. "Take this one here at Beeston. It's massive! Other weir pools are smaller and easier to fish, but here I'll concentrate on four main areas as I'll have four rods set up (and two rod licences, of course!)"

There are so many places to target on large weir pools and all are worth a cast or two. Here's where Adam cast his baits:

Area 1: Right under the bottom sill of the weir where the water under the surface will actually be quite calm. Lots of food will collect here and the fish will follow.

Area 2: In fast water a little below the bottom sill. This is another good holding spot.

Area 3: To the far side of any rocks visible at or just below the surface. This is another good area although you will need to be careful with your casting.

Area 4: Close to a very large tree that had become lodged close to the concrete wall at the base of the weir.

Beef Up Your Tackle

It is a fact that weir pools are full of snags. Many are naturally occurring, such as rocks or dead trees wedged on the bottom, but there will also be a large amount of other items washed down in the current plus, of course,

Pva-Bag Feeder

1 Pop a dry feeder into a solid PVA bag.

2 Add your feed. A mix of broken boilies and pellets is best.

3 Seal the bag around the feeder, attach to the rig and cast!

Adam's Tackle

Rods: 3lb 12ft 30Plus Radar
Reel: Shimano Ultegra Tribal 5500
Main line: 15lb Gardner Hydro Tuff
Hook link: 30Plus Big Fish rig
Feeder: 30Plus Barbel Feeder

broken tackle.

Taking this into consideration, you need to use strong tackle in weir pools. Adam's rod had a 3lb test curve and he used 15lb line. He also had a few words to say about avoiding snags.

"First, don't cast among rocks. That's asking for trouble. In low-water conditions, you'll be able to see the rocks like you can here at Beeston, but even if they're covered, a careful look will often reveal an area of broken water signalling their presence underneath.

"I always use a 1m length of leadcore above my feeder. This is far more resilient and resistant to abrasion than any monofilament.

"Also, fish with your rod high off the water. The more line you can keep out of the weir pool, the less chance there is of snagging."

Even assuming your fishing area is free from snags, all that can change when you hook a fish, and even the best of anglers will occasionally see everything become solid on the strike.

First thing to do if a fish

becomes snagged is to alter the angle of the rod. The strong current will often do the job of releasing the tackle or the fish from the snag.

Another thing to try is to put the rod back in the rests and leave it for several minutes. Again, nature will often do its work and the fish will become free.

Finally – and this is something to do only with extreme care, and never if you're by yourself – you can wade out to the area and free the tackle yourself. This is obviously dependent on the depth of the water and strength of the current.

A large open-ended feeder and a very strong hooklength of either braid or fluorocarbon finish the rig, fluorocarbon being Adam's first choice in clear water.

The feeder – or heavy gripper lead if the river is flooded – was free-running on the leadcore, stopped with a tail rubber slid over the top of a swivel joining the leadcore to the hook link. The idea of the rig is always to keep as smooth a link as possible between all of its components.

Finally, it's worth carrying a large baitdropper in your kit. This can be used to feed an area right under your rod top if the swim allows.

Weir-Pool Baits

Halibut pellets and boilies are the only things worth considering when it comes to fishing weir pools, and Adam's rules are simple. In summer, he'll feed mostly pellets, but will increase the number of boilies he feeds as the season progresses.

Hook bait is either a hair-rigged large halibut pellet or a boilie, and he'll generally recast only after landing a fish. Weir-pool fishing is a waiting game, but it's worth it when the rod goes.

"Five years ago, 14mm to 21mm halibut pellets were the only hook baits I used," said Adam. "But more recently I've been using boilies and have found that yellow ones are good. Now I'll always have a yellow boilie on at least one of my rods, and that's normally the one that'll go. In fact, my last five barbel have all been taken on yellow boilies."

Adam had to wait until late afternoon for his second and final barbel of the session.

Summer chubbing

Try this fine brace of rigs as you target flowing water for summer chub.

Short Waggler

Catching chub from a river using shallow waggler tactics is one of summer's great joys and this is the rig to use for it.

Choose a dumpy, clear, loaded waggler that's easily heavy enough to cast to your fishing spot and fix only a single shot down the line between float and hook.

You can attach the float to the line with shot either side but here we are using two float stops, which can be moved up and down the line with no chance of line damage.

This is a great rig to use with plenty of loose-fed maggots or casters, and two grubs on the hook. Feed in front, cast a little downstream and those chub will come! Alter your depth regularly.

Short, clear, loaded waggler fixed on the line with two float stops

Single No 8 shot down the line

Double maggot or caster hook bait

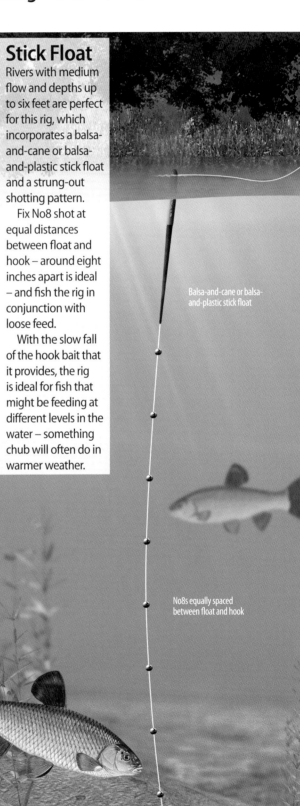

Stick Float

Rivers with medium flow and depths up to six feet are perfect for this rig, which incorporates a balsa-and-cane or balsa-and-plastic stick float and a strung-out shotting pattern.

Fix No8 shot at equal distances between float and hook – around eight inches apart is ideal – and fish the rig in conjunction with loose feed.

With the slow fall of the hook bait that it provides, the rig is ideal for fish that might be feeding at different levels in the water – something chub will often do in warmer weather.

Balsa-and-cane or balsa-and-plastic stick float

No8s equally spaced between float and hook

All-out crucian attack!

A 3lb-plus crucian carp is a real challenge, and to catch one Alan Stagg is getting a little aggressive – with his approach, that is!

Total Coarse Fishing deputy editor Steve Martin wanted a big crucian bagged live in front of the cameras. Not content with a 2lb fish, though, Steve upped the stakes and wanted a fish weighing over 3lb!

Specimen Proportions

With just a day session in which to achieve this target the choice of venue would be critical. Over the previous six weeks I had been winkling a few decent crucians from Johnson's Lake on the Marsh Farm complex, controlled by Godalming Angling Society. This 21-acre venue holds a

wide range of species, such as carp, tench and a head of cracking crucians that run to specimen proportions. This seemed to be the obvious place to start and with such a large lake to target location was going to be vital.

Conditions leading up to the day were warm with temperatures well above 20°C. A slight breeze was pushing into the shallow arm of the lake that offered an obvious ambush point and it was here where I decided to form my attack. Arriving at the fishery at dawn, Steve and I headed for this arm and I soon had my kit set up in a wide swim that allowed me to intercept fish moving

Alan Stagg

Hometown: Basingstoke
Sponsors: Gardner Tackle, Sonubaits, Enterprise Tackle
Occupation: Gardner Tackle employee
PB crucian: 4lb 2oz

Johnson's Lake Fact File

Location: Station Lane, Milford, Surrey GU8 5AE
Information: Call the tackle shop at Marsh Farm on 01483 428885
Membership: Senior – £70 plus a £65 entry fee
Website: www. godalminganglingsociety. co.uk

The Spod Mix

1 Mix 50/50 of the groundbaits, plus a handful of each of the pellets and a little added flavouring.

2 The result is a fine feed mix with small particles to get the fish looking for bigger bites.

3 Loosely load a large spod to the top with the feed mix.

4 Now compress the mix, but not too hard or it won't explode out when it hits the water.

The best of the bunch came halfway through the frantic session.

The Business End

1 With a sharp pair of scissors cut off 10 inches of 5lb Target fluorocarbon.

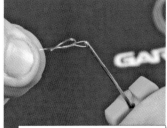

2 Tie a simple double-overhand knot and pull tight.

3 Thread on your hook bait, in this case a 6mm pellet.

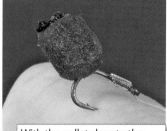

4 With the pellet close to the bend of the hook, tie a simple knotless knot to finish the rig.

Alan's Top Five Tips For Catching A 3lb Crucian

1 Flat-bed Method feeders certainly seem to trick these crafty fish.

2 Accuracy is vital in feeder fishing; use a stop knot in conjunction with the reel's line clip.

3 Don't be afraid to be aggressive in this style of fishing. The fish aren't shy of lots of bait and this will help hold them in the swim.

4 Cast regularly. If the rods haven't received any action after 15 minutes then recast. Bites will often come soon after.

5 Small 6mm Sonubaits S-Pellets make deadly hook baits.

to and from this area. I knew from past experience that I didn't need to fish far out and that a comfortable 20-yard cast into three feet of water was all that was required.

Stop-Knot Marker

A quick cast with a Method feeder, slowly inching it across the bottom, revealed that the lake bed was clear.

I quickly placed the line in the spool's line clip before reeling in. I paced this along the bank and repeated this procedure with my other rod and a spod rod, to ensure I would be fishing as accurately as possible. I added a stop-knot marker to the reel lines, which would allow me to hit the desired distance when a fish was landed or I needed to recast.

A Fine Feed Mix

I had mixed my groundbait the evening before and

decided on a fine mix made from Sonubaits F1 Dark and Supercrush Green mixed 50/50. I added very few feed items to the groundbait, just a sprinkling of 2mm S-Pellets and a pinch of Sonubaits 4mm Elliptical Pellets. The idea was to form a lot of attraction and smell in the water with very few large items for the fish to fill themselves up on.

I started the session aggressively and introduced around 30 Bait Rockets of groundbait. I had

Who would not be smiling after catching this brace of 3lb-plus fish.

deliberately mixed it quite dry so that it would explode out of the spod, forming an attractive cloud through the water column.

A String Of Small Tench

Soon after the initial bombardment, I had two small 30g flat Method feeders deposited accurately on the baited patch. Each contained a hair-rigged 6mm Sonubaits S-Pellet as hook bait, as previous sessions had demonstrated how effective these could be.

When using small Method feeders I always recast regularly, usually every 15 minutes. Bites will often come quickly after recasting as the fish home in on the feeder. After several recasts my bite alarm signalled the first action of the day. The next hour saw a string of small tench landed, all around 1lb to 2lb in weight.

Aggressive Style

From previous experience I knew these little critters could eat a lot of bait, and I wanted to feed them off and give the crucians a chance of finding my baited patch. As I carried on bombarding the swim with bait Steve looked slightly surprised by the aggressive style I had adopted.

Within 10 minutes a further bite had me playing what felt very different from the characteristic fight from the tench I had been plagued with. It was no surprise when the golden flanks of a crucian carp surfaced and was led over the waiting net. A lovely plump specimen was soon being unhooked and, weighing 2lb 12oz, it was a good start to the day but short of my target weight.

A Hectic Session

Over the next six hours the swim went into overdrive, as crucian after crucian

fell to the rods. When not recasting I was playing a fish or re-baiting – the action was hectic, to say to the least, and at one point I couldn't get two rods out in the water!

In that period a total of 20 crucians (and the odd small invasive tench) fell to the rods, with seven – yes, seven – fish weighing over the magical 3lb mark. The best three fish were two at 3lb 3oz and one weighing 3lb 3oz 8dr.

It was a fantastic day's fishing, one that you dream about, but the conditions were spot-on, and I doubt that it will happen for the cameras again.

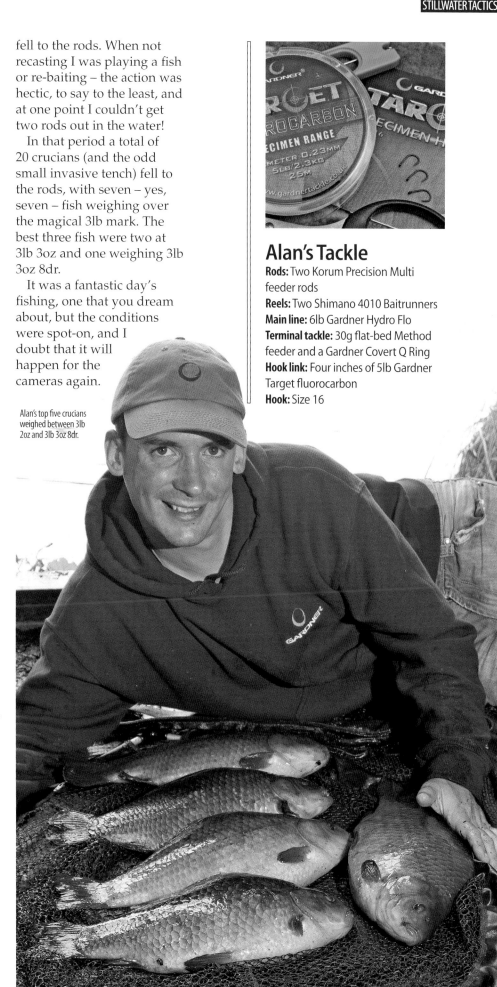

Alan's top five crucians weighed between 3lb 2oz and 3lb 3oz 8dr.

Alan's Tackle

Rods: Two Korum Precision Multi feeder rods
Reels: Two Shimano 4010 Baitrunners
Main line: 6lb Gardner Hydro Flo
Terminal tackle: 30g flat-bed Method feeder and a Gardner Covert Q Ring
Hook link: Four inches of 5lb Gardner Target fluorocarbon
Hook: Size 16

Top rigs for bream

Bream will feed at all times of the year. Here are four great rigs to use for a big catch on river or lake.

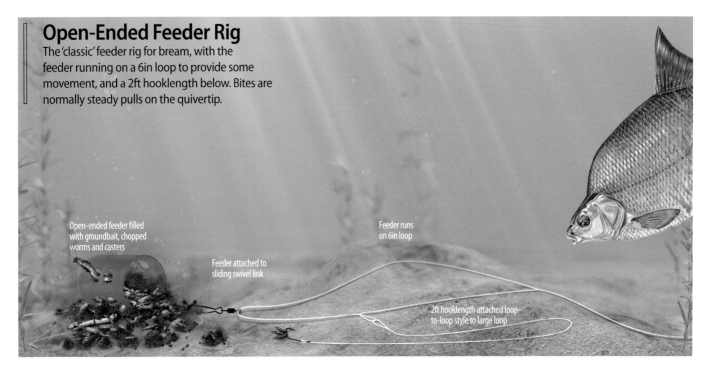

Open-Ended Feeder Rig

The 'classic' feeder rig for bream, with the feeder running on a 6in loop to provide some movement, and a 2ft hooklength below. Bites are normally steady pulls on the quivertip.

Open-ended feeder filled with groundbait, chopped worms and casters

Feeder attached to sliding swivel link

Feeder runs on 6in loop

2ft hooklength attached loop-to-loop style to large loop

Straight Paternoster Rig

The simplest of rigs, and one that has probably caught more bream than any other. Use a tail length of between two and three feet and feed balls of groundbait, loose feed or even use a spod to introduce particles where you're casting.

Leger attached to 6in link and tied to main line with water knot

2ft to 3ft hooklength attached loop-to-loop style to main line

Slider Rig

A great float rig for deep waters where you need to get the bait down to the bottom quickly. Fish with the bait just touching bottom, or a few inches overdepth in windy conditions.

Sliding stop knot

Loaded, bodied slider

Bulk of BBs or AAAs 3ft from hook

No4

No4

Hook bait can be fished just touching bottom or several inches overdepth if windy

Float-leger Rig

Try this rig on lakes using a small Method or open-ended feeder and a Polaris float, which slides up the line before locking in place once the feeder lands on the bottom.

Polaris float attached to 5lb main line

Flat Method feeder fished semi-bolt style with buffer bead and swivel pushed inside

3in hooklength of 3lb mono

No strings attached!

We delve into the mind of angling's leading innovator, Andy Findlay, to discover how and why he invented the banjo feeder.

Andy Findlay can afford a smile as he nets a 6lb carp on a freezing day. The sharpest mind in match fishing has done it again, adding another successful invention to his long list of achievements. It's no wonder he's sponsored by a company with 'Innovations' in its name…

Even Preston Innovations sometimes finds it hard to keep up with the man who just can't stop, well, innovating.

"I think sometimes they hate it when I ring them with a new idea," he jokes. "Not really, of course, but it usually means lots of work getting it made."

Andy has been a thinker ever since he first became interested in angling, fishing the tough Eastern match circuit on places like the River Nene's famous North Bank, near Peterborough.

As his beloved rivers declined and match anglers turned to the fast-growing commercial-fishery circuit, Andy followed suit, and his inquiring mind was soon working overtime.

"Commercial fisheries were a whole new thing and they gave me the perfect opportunity to get my thinking head on to try to stay one step ahead," he says. Now, commercial anglers – and not just match men either – can thank Andy for many of the products they use every week.

The pellet feeder – Andy invented it. The cone – that was also down to Andy. The flat Method – Andy again. The list goes on.

"The pellet feeder is a good example of how I come up with things," he reveals. "Basically, I'd caught loads of carp using conventional open-ended-feeder tactics, casting to islands and into open water. So had a lot of other anglers, so it was hardly surprising that the carp eventually became wary and catches started to tail off on many commercials.

"I thought long and hard about this and came up with a feeder with one sloping end into which both dampened pellets and, importantly, my hook bait could be squeezed. My first versions didn't look very professional but I knew

Andy Findlay
Hometown: Leicester
Sponsors: Preston Innovations, Sonubaits

Andy's Banjo Feed

1 Fin Perfect 1mm feed pellets and One to One Paste from Sonubaits.

2 Add two small tubs of pellets and one of dry paste mix to a bowl.

3 Two tubs of water are added and the mix swirled around.

4 Thirty minutes later, the finished result.

The banjo feeder: Perfect for venues where the carp are Method-wary.

I was onto a winner when I landed 171lb of carp the first time I used it. I was catching the big, old fish as well, fish that hadn't been seen in numbers on the lake for ages. They hadn't been seen because no-one had caught them! It needed something different to fool them.

"The thing about the pellet feeder, and this is the key with all my inventions, was that it was different. It wasn't some magical fish-catcher that conjured up carp from nowhere. It simply provided the carp with food they wanted to eat, in a way that didn't make them suspicious, a way they'd never seen before. For a while anyway!

"Once Preston Innovations made it and released it on to the market, I knew I'd soon have to think of something else! It's still a brilliant fish-catcher, though, and I'm still winning with it regularly at places like Makins and Packington. For pleasure anglers, it's a fantastic way of fishing against islands."

Play That Banjo

The banjo feeder is Andy's latest invention. Well, the latest one he's prepared to talk about – he's certainly got others tucked away in the drawer marked 'top secret!' So how did he come up with this one?

"The process was a similar one to the pellet feeder, to be truthful," he explains. "Flat Method feeders have dominated for several years where they're allowed, and I'm glad to see that most commercials now do allow them. And why shouldn't they?

"However, on those lakes where the flat Method had been used a lot, I knew its effectiveness would eventually start to wane. Even though the flat Method still catches tons of carp, I wanted something that presented my bait in a slightly different way."

Loading The Banjo Feeder

1 Make sure the feeder is wet.

2 Add a little mix and place the hook bait on it.

3 Add another layer of feed.

4 Squeeze against your palm to compress.

5 Ready for casting.

That wasn't easy. What could be better than having a hook bait right in among a neat pile of groundbait, pellets, or both, slowly melting away from the feeder to be revealed as the most attractive morsel inside?

What Andy came up with, he reckons, now provides a presentation of feed and hook bait that's better even than the Method.

"For a start, it's different, which I've already said is so important when you're fishing for wary carp. But the banjo is more than that. I reckon it actually improves on the Method when it comes to presenting a hook bait among pellets and groundbait."

Now the banjo is Andy's first choice of feeder for open-water fishing, especially in winter when the water is cold.

So what are the advantages of the banjo over the flat Method feeder?

"Generally speaking, the banjo holds less feed than a Method feeder. It's perfect when the fish don't want too much feed," Andy explains. "With the Method, there's enough bait on the feeder for probably four or five fish. The banjo is different, though. There's only enough feed for one fish to be kept occupied, and that's exactly what you want in winter. I've found it's fantastic for slowly building up a swim through small consignments of feed.

"The banjo also casts brilliantly – better than the Method – and I've found I can use a smaller and lighter feeder and still get casting accuracy, which has got to be a good thing for wary carp.

"Furthermore, I've done masses of tank tests, and as long as the water is more than 12 inches deep, the banjo lands on the lake bed the right way up, every single time.

"The most important difference, though, is the way the feed 'looks' on the bottom. What you get with the banjo is a neat, round pile of feed with your hook bait sitting right in among it. The idea is that a carp roots around this feed, finds your hook bait and takes it without hesitation. There are no plastic ribs to scare a fish away either."

At first, Preston Innovations wasn't too keen on making the product considering it was enjoying great success with Andy's recently introduced flat Method feeders.

However, persuaded by Andy that the flat Method

Andy prefers elasticated banjos, where allowed, as fish losses are reduced with these.

Andy has found that the banjo feeder catches the biggest fish, that have seen it all before.

and the banjo could be sold alongside each other, with benefits for each, the company released them in 2011… and sold them in their thousands.

"I wasn't too unhappy that Preston didn't rush to release them," he laughs, "because I knew that I'd have the banjo to myself for a bit longer!"

First time out with a home-made version saw 163lb of carp fall to the banjo. After that, he tried it on several different venues, including one memorable match at Naseby Reservoir where he caught 90lb for second place from a no-hope peg.

"That was the day that convinced me the banjo had a place. I was certain I

> *The most important difference is the way the feed looks on the bottom.*

wouldn't have caught on other methods."

Bait

Andy's feed is a combination of two parts Sonubaits Fin Perfect 1mm feed pellets, one part Sonubaits One to One paste mix and two parts water. Put it all into a bowl, swirl it around, and leave it for half an hour, then simply mix it with your hands.

Andy prefers to add it to his feeder in small amounts, covering the bottom initially, then adding his hook bait – either a hair-rigged piece of punched polony or a Sonubaits S-Pellet on a 3in hooklength – and a final layer of the paste-and-pellet mix.

Andy's Session

A short session with the banjo at Makins Fishery saw Andy land a succession of carp to 10lb plus some fine bream. He used the elasticated version of the feeder rather than an inline one, as with the elasticated one he could prepare another one on his side tray and simply swap it for the empty feeder after landing a fish. You can't do this with an inline feeder. Every fish fell to a 6mm piece of hair-rigged polony.

On a bitterly cold day, when several other anglers on Lake One struggled for a bite, Andy certainly showed that this banjo certainly has no strings attached!

Commercial lakes

Where should you fish on a commercial lake? That's the problem faced by thousands of anglers every weekend at their local day-ticket fishery.

Underwater Features
Take advantage of these. Species like carp, F1s and chub will all be found close to them. Tackle them with a feeder or waggler.

Upper Layers
In warm weather, F1s, carp and silver fish will all feed readily close to the surface, where they can be tackled with pole tackle and casters.

Deep Holes
Careful plumbing might reveal deeper places in your swim. These will be highly productive in the winter for carp and bream.

Commercial fisheries can look very similar from above the surface. However, under the water there are often just as many features as there are on more natural venues.

The margins, drop-offs, shelves, slopes, islands, reeds, weeds, lilies… all of these are present in commercials, acting as fish-attractors, and a good angler will know which areas to target at different times of the year.

Think about water depth. In the warmer months, species like carp, F1s and chub will certainly be feeding in the upper layers and a shallow pole approach can work well for these. The margins, meanwhile, will also hold fish in the summer, especially late in the day.

However, when the water starts to cool down, you need to concentrate more on the deeper water. Plumb the depth carefully and fish in any slightly deeper areas for carp and bream.

Other species such as roach, rudd and ide will often be found in commercials and can provide great winter sport to anglers fishing simple waggler tactics with maggots on the hook.

Follow our guide to what to look for on a typical commercial swim.

Bottom Of Near Slope

This area of your swim will often produce carp at some point during the session. Sweetcorn and luncheon meat are the best baits here, but feed sparingly.

The Margins

Feed these all day and expect to catch in as little as a foot of water. Watch for signs of fish. Excellent late in the day.

Go live for big perch

Arctic-like weather fails to discourage predator ace Mick Brown, as he goes livebaiting for big perch.

Whatever the size, perch cannot resist a small, trotted livebait.

You can catch river perch at any time during the season, but as the baitfish shoal up when winter comes, the specimens start to strike.

I look forward to the first decent rainfall in late autumn. It adds a little colour to the river, making presentation less critical. The extra pace seems to bring the river alive and further aids presentation, by allowing baits to be trotted in the flow. Any time from early December through to the end of the river season, you are likely to find me travelling light along the banks of the tributaries of my local fenland rivers in search of perch.

My realistic target is a two-pounder. In this day and age when the weeklies seem to be regularly full of specimen perch, it's important to realise that a 2lb fish is still a good size target fish, and very few venues, or anglers, are regularly turning up bigger specimens. Quite often, we are simply reading about the same fish being caught over and over again, from venues like the upper Great Ouse. So, for me, a two-pounder makes my day, and a three-pounder in the net is still, as far as I'm concerned, a red-letter day. A 3lb perch really is a fantastic fish to catch.

Additional Tackle

There are many ways of tackling these venues, and I am usually armed with a few options. Certainly, small lures are very viable, and in milder conditions all I will take is a light lure outfit and half a dozen trusted lures. These include a size 6 Mepps spinner, a fat-bodied plug like a Rapala Fat Rap or the good old Shakespeare Midi 'S', a ½oz spinner bait like the Fox Hornet and a 4in jig with an 18g jighead.

If I know where there are plenty of perch holed up and it's not too cold, I'll just take a match rod, made up with a suitable stick float, and lay on overdepth with a lobworm, baiting the swim with a groundbait/liquid worm/chopped worm mix, and sit it out for the day. When it gets bitterly cold, though, as it did when I set out to catch a perch for the camera, and I'm pretty convinced that the other tactics aren't going to work, I will switch to the best perch bait of all – a small livebait! I could, of course, use such a tactic at any time, but it's a lot more trouble to go to, as first of all you have to catch some livebait. This means additional tackle and bait, making the tackle more bulky, but I accept there are times when this is the only way to go.

Find The Features

For this feature session, it couldn't really have been any colder, with an overnight fall of snow, which quickly

Mick Brown
Hometown: Market Deeping, Lincs
Sponsors: Shimano, Rapala, Dynamite Baits

froze and set solid, making walking the riverbank very treacherous. To catch a 2lb perch for the camera was now not just a target, but more of a challenge, which I knew was achievable if I could locate a swim that held some perch.

The sort of swims I was looking for could easily be described by their features. Alongside moored boats, under bridges, deeper holes in the river and anywhere with features such as pump outlets, vertical banking and fallen trees. These were the sort of places I was after, but they must hold one more vital ingredient – shoals of smaller prey fish. Always remember, a swim that looks good isn't necessarily going to be good, it has to have ALL the right ingredients, the most vital of all being an ample food supply. If I can catch livebaits from the swim with relative ease, then I can usually be fairly confident that there will be some decent perch among them.

So, my first objective of the day was to catch a few small livebaits, and by small I was thinking of fish from three to four inches. Any silver fish is ideal, but I'm just as happy to use small perch, ruffe or gudgeon if that's all that's available. Usually, though, swims holding good numbers of silver fish offer the best chances. Years of fishing smaller rivers has taught me a vital lesson; the perch and the prey will not be evenly spread over the river, but tightly

shoaled in often quite small areas. The colder it becomes, it seems, the tighter these areas also become.

Short Stops

Winter days can be very short and a process of trial and error in finding decent swims needs to be carried out quickly and efficiently. Knowing that many swims can be totally barren, I will rarely spend more than half an hour checking them out.

It's easy to get carried away into thinking that a lack of bites mean there's a need to refine the tackle, but I believe that much of the time, the lack of bites means that there are no fish in the area. If I can't get a bite on a size 18 hook to a 1.1lb bottom, with a single maggot on the hook, then I'm even more convinced that this isn't a swim worth spending much time on. With this in mind, I travelled light with just my livebait bucket to sit on, a small haversack to carry a few bits and pieces, and my food and drink for the session.

Telltale Signs

It would have been easy to give up on this session, as after two moves I hadn't had a single bite when running a stick float down the swim, just tripping bottom with a single maggot. After my second move, though, in the far distance I noticed a couple of small fry flip out of the water next to a moored boat, and as I made my way towards it, I noticed another small fish

jump out, which made me quicken my pace. As I found a gap between a couple of near-bank moored boats, I noticed a definite giveaway close to the hull of a boat moored on the far bank, which told me that perch were active – bubbles! Perch often chase small fish to the surface, and as they strike make a distinctive swirl with a few bubbles in it. I definitely saw a perch make an attack, and noted another small fish flap near the hull of the boat. This was a swim I needed to explore to try and winkle a perch out.

Mick's Float Tip

To ensure a clean strike when a fish takes the bait, Mick coats the line above his float with grease or floatant to stop the line from sinking.

Mick's Mix

1 Brown crumb and a little liquid worm will attract both predators and prey.

2 Pour a small amount of groundbait, about half a bag, into a large bait tub.

3 To give the mix a meaty flavour, Mick adds a few squirts of the liquid worm…

4 … before adding a little water (or snow, in this case) and mixing well.

5 You need a firm, but dry mix that's easy to throw, but quickly breaks up.

Big perch love the cover of features like boats to set their ambush.

Mick's Livebait Rig

16g sliding pole float

10lb mono main line

Two SSG shot attached to the top of the wire trace

10in trace of 20lb seven-strand wire

Small silver fish on a size 4 wide-gape hook

I shallowed up and cast across into the shadow of the far-bank boat. It zoomed away almost instantly, and I got my first livebait, a 4in bleak – the perfect perch bait.

Adapted Tackle

My perch rod was actually my barbel gear – a 1.75lb test curve rod and a 4000-size reel loaded with 10lb mono. It's slightly overgunned, but the chances of a pike taking it were very likely and the tackle needed to be up to landing it, should this happen.

My float was a 16g Sensas slider, but in the shallow water I was fishing – no more than seven feet deep – I liked the simplicity of using it as a fixed float, locked by a top rubber. I find this easier to adjust in cold weather than a sliding knot. At the business end, I had a 10in wire trace made from 20lb seven-strand wire, unfortunately needed where pike are likely, especially on Fenland rivers. I'd certainly catch a lot more perch without the wire trace. A couple of SSG shots were pinched onto the trace, to cock the float and get the bait down. The hook was a size 4 wide-gape carp pattern. I use a barbed version for winter fishing. At times when the perch are bolting the baits down, I will use a barbless hook.

The livebait was lightly hooked through the top lip, and when using a barbed hook, I slip a small piece of elastic band over the point and barb, to reduce the chances of the bait coming adrift on the cast. For barbless hooks, I use a slightly longer piece of elastic band stretched between the shank and the point to achieve the same effect.

Bites In Slow Motion

Catching a big perch will never be about the fight. They are not great fighters. For me, it's more about the excitement of the bite and the anticipation, as the fish shows itself at the landing net. If it feels heavy, you suspect a pike, but the thought of a big

Mick's Livebait Tip

Mick uses a big, size 4 hook when targeting perch, so to reduce the chances of the bait coming adrift on the cast, he slips a small piece of elastic band over the point and barb.

perch is always in the back of your mind. When it is, panic often sets in, as they always appear bigger than they are in the water!

I soon had half a dozen small baits in my bucket, and I was ready to send one down through the swim. On the first run down I fished just off bottom. This resulted in a typical perch bite, as the float just slipped away in slow motion. A quick strike and I missed it! It was another half a dozen runs through before I had another take. This time I latched into it, and even though it weighed less than 1lb, I was happy to have got some sort of a result, as the water really was icy cold and the skies were blackening, as another bout of bad weather approached from the north.

Encouraged To Feed

Two more missed runs told me that the perch weren't all that enthusiastic. I

decided to give them a bit of encouragement in the form of a cloud groundbait, to get the prey fish excited and darting and flashing about. I quickly mixed a couple of handfuls of brown crumb and a good squirt of liquidised worm – a proven perch attractor. I like to make the feed as sloppy as possible, but to get it to the far bank I had to make it a little firmer. Half a dozen small balls were introduced to the swim, making them hit the water with a splash to break them up and small fish were obviously excited by its introduction, as a few started breaking the surface to nip at the floating crumbs.

That's No 'Jack'!

Two more runs through the swim failed to produce, so I changed to a tactic, that works not just for perch, but pike and zander too in very cold weather. Knowing the bottom was fairly clean, I set the float

about a foot overdepth. This held up the bait, so it was slowly dragged along the bottom.

On the first run, the float slid away in a very decisive manner, and as I struck, the bend in the rod convinced me that a jack pike had taken the bait. However, as I drew the fish closer to my big net I caught the first sign of a big perch. What a cracker! Its colourful flanks glinted in the weak winter sunshine as it entered the net. It weighed a little short of 3lb, but it made my day, justifying being out in the coldest of conditions. Mission accomplished!

By following my simple approach, anyone can catch perch like this. In many parts of the country such fish tend to be neglected. Pick the right river conditions, find the prey fish and tackle up correctly and there's every chance you will catch a few. It's not rocket science and it's great fun!

This near-3lb perch wasn't put off the feed by the arctic conditions. Mission accomplished Mick!

Feed hard, fish harder!

Bob James tackles a traditional-looking, lily-packed stillwater, but there's nothing old-school about his approach…

Bob James
Hometown: Downton
Sponsor: Richworth

Bob bagged nine tench and four bream from the deeper water at the edge of the lilies.

When an angler arrives at a natural lake, with reed-fringed margins and large beds of lilies in the centre of the pool it can only conjure up one thought – tench. That was certainly in the mind of Bob James as he arrived at a favourite East Anglian fishery for an early morning rendezvous with deputy editor Steve Martin. However, any thoughts of Bob fishing traditional tactics went out of the window as he unpacked his tackle and bait for the day, then put the camping stove on for an early morning cuppa and bacon sandwich before things got serious.

Steve Martin *Nice cuppa and sarnie, Bob! A first look at your kit and all that bait indicates that you're expecting to catch big fish today, but considering the venue it's not exactly geared towards traditional tactics.*

Bob James When you start the day this early you have to be in the right mood, and a cup of tea and a bacon sandwich is just what you need.

There are some cracking tench, bream and carp in this lake, so light tackle isn't an option, especially with all those lilies in front of me. Another reason is I'm fishing Method-style, so I need the tackle to cast the heavy feed ball.

SM *Can you talk me through the details of your setup?*
BJ I'm doubling up today using identical 12ft barbel rods – these are ideal for big tench and bream – each with a freespool reel loaded with 8lb line. At the business end I have a free-running, weighted Method feeder, stopped by a swivel and buffer bead. I'm using a size 10 hook attached to a short hook link, with a long hair to take two mini-boilies.

SM *I've also noticed you are fishing bobbins as well as bite alarms. Bites on the Method are normally very positive, so why the bobbins?*
BJ They help distinguish between line bites and proper takes. A fish passing under the line will cause the bobbin to rise and fall, as it rubs against it. Bream especially, as they have such a big back, can pull the line a lot, so I won't strike unless the bobbin hits the rod and stays there!

SM *As you are fishing the Method, I assume your groundbait mix is going to be heavy and sticky?*
BJ I'm using a mixture of three Richworth products – K-G-1 Bag and Stick mix, Super Method XL groundbait (the sweet mix) and K-G-1 Multi-Stim Pellets. These are full of the attractants and sweet-smelling flavours, which tench and bream love.

Feeding Tip
Bob closes the mouth of his large pouch catapult around the boilies before firing, so that they land in a tight group.

Hair-Rig Tip
Bob ties an extra-long hair to enable him to fish a doubled-up bait when the fish are in a feeding mood.

Bob's heavy feed bombardment ensured a hectic morning's action from quality tench and bream.

However, it makes a fairly light mix, which doesn't require too much water to make it sticky.

SM *Do you mix the separate*

Feed Like Bob James!

1 Bob uses half a bag of each of the mixes and pellets.

2 These are thoroughly mixed dry in a large bowl.

3 Once mixed and wetted, Bob creates 10 orange-sized balls.

4 These are then fed to the edge of the lilies.

5 Two or three pouches of boilies are added over the top.

groundbaits first or all three feeds at once, as the pellets are the hard type?

BJ All together! I just add the same amount of each to a large mixing bowl, giving it a good shake while it's dry to blend them together, and then I add the water, leaving it to soak in after the first mixing. The pellets normally start to soften quickly. After about 10 minutes I'll add more water until the mix feels right and then I'll leave it to finish the absorption process.

SM *You mentioned you were fishing mini-boilies today as hook baits. Do you have a favourite choice, as there are*

loads to choose from these days?

BJ Obviously I want to be fishing a bait that's a similar flavour to my feed, so I'm using Richworth's 10mm K-G-1 baits. I will admit that these are a bit of a favourite of mine, as they catch pretty much most of the specimen fish I like to target – barbel, chub, tench, bream and carp. And because they are a soft bait, there's no need to mess about with a bait drill. And to make the baits even more appealing, I spray them with K-G-1 liquid.

SM *You pointed out the mass of lilies in front of you earlier. Is that your target area today?*

BJ There are two areas that

I'm going to feed – the first is just to the right, and in front of the patch, which stretches furthermost out into the lake. The second is to the left of that, where the lilies create a sort of 'bay'. These areas are where the deeper water starts and where I would expect the fish to patrol, looking for trapped food at the edge of the drop-off.

SM *Well, it looks like you're ready for the off. Will you feed first or just cast out both rods with loaded feeders?*

BJ You know me – I'll feed first. I want to get plenty of food out there to get the fish on the feed. I've spotted a few bubbles rising – a good

Bob's Bait
- 1x bag of Richworth K-G-1 Bag & Stick Mix
- 1 x bag of Richworth Super Method Fish Mix
- 1 x bag of Richworth K-G-1 Multi-Stim Pellets
- 2 x bags of Richworth K-G-1 10mm boilies

Bob's Gear
- 12ft travel barbel rod
- 4000-size freespool reel
- 8lb reel line
- 28g Method feeder
- Size 12 hook

indication that the fish are grubbing about, but I want to give them something to really get them going.

SM *So how much are you going to feed?*
BJ In a word – loads! I'm going to feed 10 big balls of groundbait in each area, followed by the same amount of loose-fed boilies. That will get them interested. Also, I'll wait a while after feeding, until I get positive signs that the fish are over the bait and eating. Well, you have to make time for another cup of tea! Once they start to feed, it's then just a case of casting in over their heads. And rather than spook the fish, I find that the feeder stimulates the fish even more.

SM *Will you re-feed during the day, or rely on what's around the Method feeder once you start fishing?*
BJ There are a lot of fish in this lake, and once they get feeding I'm sure they will soon hoover up what I feed, so yes, I will keep topping up with plenty of groundbait and boilies on a regular basis.

A good sign that I may need to top will be a sudden reduction in bubbles breaking the surface. That's always a big clue that the food supply has run out.

SM *You're certainly fishing very positively today. However, would this tactic work on other venues that are not as prolific?*
BJ It certainly works on lakes where there is a large head of tench or bream, but you will need to do the homework to find out if a water is heavily populated like this one. I can think of a few – Frensham Ponds in Surrey is one, Richworth Linear Fisheries in Oxfordshire another. Bury Hill Fisheries in Dorking will also respond to a positive approach like the one I'm using today.

Tench were the early morning feeders.

The specimen bream showed up later.

There's always one carp!

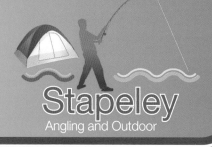

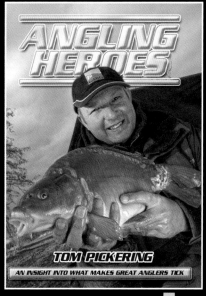
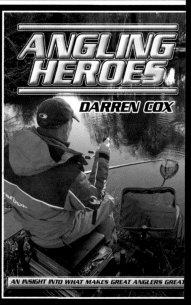

Accessorise Your Chair!

Add seatbox-type accessories to you chair with the new 30 Plus Multi-Chair Leg Adaptor for stress-free fishing.

There's nothing more relaxing than spending a day on the bank of your local fishery, just sitting back in your chair, with your eyes glued to the rod/float tip, waiting for a bite. The only trouble is, unlike with a seatbox, you are not always in direct contact with your rod, which can result in missed bites.

Most anglers find that they have to reach down or across to pick up their rod, which means a delay in striking. It would be far better to be able to drop your hand directly over the rod the instant you get a bite.

30Plus has come up with an adaptor that fixes to your chair to allow you to do just that – the Multi Chair Leg Adaptor. It's easy to attach, and once clamped around the leg of your chair it allows you to convert it into a fishing station. You can add numerous accessories, including feeder arms, trays and rod rests, plus a lot more – visit www.specimen30plus.com for the full range.

Once the adaptor is fitted it will neatly fold away when not in use and does not stop a chair folding down for transportation. It's a brilliant little gadget that should have been thought of years ago!

The Multi Chair Adaptor is available from all good 30Plus stockists.

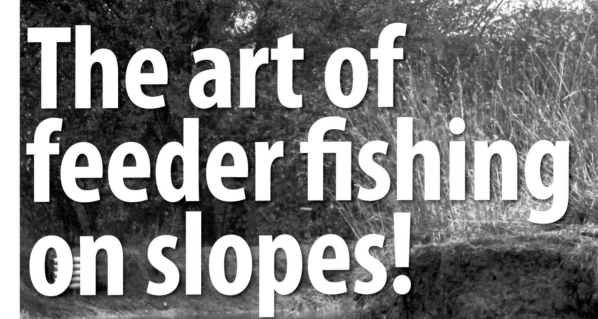

The art of feeder fishing on slopes!

Do you think enough about the weight of your feeder when you're fishing close to islands? Alan Scotthorne believes you could improve your results overnight by following his simple advice.

Islands are key fish-holding areas. But are you getting the most from every cast?

Alan packs his bait onto a Method feeder as hard as he can, so it reaches the lake bed intact.

The Perfect Press

1 The aim is to have a hook bait here. So…

2 … three-quarters fill the mould with bait…

3 … place your hook bait right here…

4 … and press it into the feed.

Being five-times world champion doesn't happen by accident. It stems from a life committed to angling with every aspect considered, reconsidered and perfected. The subject of feeder fishing to islands is one area where Alan believes many anglers could improve to boost their weights, literally, overnight – sounds simple enough!

It's all too easy to get hung up on fancy baits, flavours, perfect hooklengths, the right hooks and all of the other technical hype that goes with fishing. But, while each of these aspects has an important role to play, if we said to you that Alan Scotthorne believes that 10g of extra lead on your feeders will double your weights, no doubt your ears would prick up at the very simplicity of the statement. Over to Alan…

I've come to Cob House Fishery, in Worcester, today, for a specific purpose.

It's a superb venue with outstanding facilities, but the pool I want to fish today, Laugherne Island, features an island to cast to – typical of many commercial waters you may think. However, because the water in the lake is low (approximately three feet down) it presents the perfect opportunity to see what I'd normally be casting to when fishing tight to islands. This gives the perfect visual demonstration of one of the fundamental points I want to make – the severity of the slope!

While the slope running up to the island will vary from fishery to fishery, the key is to use a feeder heavy enough to 'stick'.

The very essence of Method-feeder fishing is to present a hook bait in the middle of a pile of feed. So, if your feeder moves for any reason you need to wind in and recast. However, you can do several things to ensure your feeder stays where you cast it.

Alan Scotthorne

Team: Ultimate Barnsley Blacks, Drennan England
Sponsor: Drennan
Lives: Rotherham

Cob House Fishery

Wichenford, Worcester
Satnav: WR6 6YE
Tel: 01886 888517
Web: *www. cobhousefisheries. co.uk*

When island slopes are very steep a heavy feeder is needed. Alan uses a 35g version here.

Sink your line very carefully to avoid moving your feeder.

Fishing a slack reel line between feeder and rod tip reduces the chance of the feeder being moved.

Alan will use a lighter 25g feeder on flatter areas of the swim as it's less likely to move.

5 Note how the hook bait is buried.

6 Place the Method feeder onto the bait.

7 Press the feeder in as hard as possible.

8 Lift the loaded feeder from the mould.

Note how Alan holds the line while sinking it.

Use a slack line from rod tip to feeder.

Alan's preferred reel line and 4000 series Baitrunner reel.

Feeder Weights

Adding weight to your feeders is a stopgap solution really, as gluing strips of lead to the feeder base causes it to sit higher off the lake bed. This isn't ideal as the perfect Method-feeder design would see the feeder laying flush to the lake bed.

I favour the latest Drennan design because they feature a low profile. They're available in various weights, meaning they cover open water and island fishing.

For today's session I've set two up – a 35g version for casting close to the island where the slope is still quite steep, and a 25g version for fishing in the open water away from the island. Were the water at its normal level I would still set the same rigs up.

The extra 10g weight will help your feeder grip the steep slope, which is absolutely vital. I would have no hesitation in increasing the weight further if the slope was steeper, or if the wind or tow was severe.

Fish movement, wafting tails, line bites, heavy wind, excessive tow and a tight line to your rod tip can all move your feeder.

Now you know this you can do something about it, which brings me nicely on to my second point.

Sinking Your Line

Line choice is important and if you don't use a line that sinks easily I'd advise you treat it with a degreaser to make it cut through the surface film. The Sufix Elite I use is silky smooth and very strong for its diameter. It also sinks quite easily straight from the spool, which helps. However, the most important element to master is the way you sink your line.

A feeder nailed to the far-bank slope resulted in a carp almost every cast!

Once you've cast your feeder to the spot IT MUST NOT MOVE until either a fish takes it, or you wind in. After the feeder has hit the lake bed sink the rod tip and hold the line (by your reel) in one hand. Tighten lightly and watch your line as it sinks.

Holding your line in this fashion allows you to feel everything that's going on and means you can feel your feeder. Once all the line is sunk put your rod carefully on the rests, ensuring you leave a small amount of slack line.

I use a 4000 series Shimano Baitrunner, and the free-spool facility is engaged to safeguard against savage takes! Another benefit of the Baitrunner facility is that I can release line off the spool easily if the wind or tow is causing the line to tighten while I'm waiting for a bite.

Moulding Your Feeder

Method moulds have brought effective Method-feeder fishing to one and all. However, there's still a knack to getting it right. You MUST press your bait on as hard as

Alan believes gluing extra lead to your feeders, like this, is not the right thing to do!

These two types of bead give a different bolt effect on the bite.

Note how much lower the feeder (left) will sit on the lake bed.

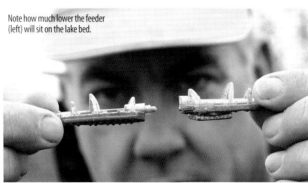

you can – I know when I've had a hectic day's Method fishing because my thumbs are sore at the end!

Pellets come off the feeder frame easily as it hits the water, but fishing to a clip so your feeder lands with a 'plop', as opposed to crashing into the lake, will prevent this to some degree. However, I believe that sometimes, no matter how hard you press, the very nature and tackiness of pellets means some come off on impact. I think many anglers actually lose their bait at this point purely through not compressing it on to the frame hard enough.

I use Horlicks to help stick my pellets together and Green Swim Stim groundbait to give a more pliable texture and a boost of extra fishmeal.

I also ensure that my hook bait is buried right inside the ball of feed – that's the way it should be!

Inline/Beads

I want to touch on the various types of setups you can use. I always opt for inline, primarily because it's accepted at every venue where the Method is allowed. Elasticated versions are banned at many waters, so I don't like to complicate my choices when I'm in a situation where I can use either.

The type of bead you use to connect your main line to hooklength is a key consideration. The Drennan Method Connectors sit in the end of the feeder and give more resistance to a fish on the take. This results in even more explosive bites than the other type I like to use – the Drennan Quick Change Bead. The Quick Change version is larger and rests on the end of the feeder as opposed to sitting inside. Venue rules dictate which I choose, but where possible I will use the former.

The Session

After a super breakfast in the on-site Mayfly café I've decided to sit on one of the pegs near the end of the island on Laugherne Island pool.

You can see from the images just how steep the initial slope is against the island. This

Top Tip

Maximise the strength of your knot by using three turns. Alan uses a Sensas Loop Tyer to form his.

Easy Assembly

1 Twizzle the last eight inches of line for strength.

2 Pass a barbed needle inside the feeder tube.

3 Hook the twizzled line onto the needle.

4 Pull through and attach your preferred bead.

Alan's simple but well-honed Method setup.

Press the bait onto the feeder frame as hard as you can!

Your pellets are perfect when you can form a sticky ball like this.

Horlicks sticks the feed pellets together, while Swim Stim adds a fishmeal boost.

proves how vital it is to use a feeder that's heavy enough to stay in place once you've cast it in.

I set up the lighter 25g version for fishing on flat bottoms because it's less likely to move compared to when you're fishing on a sloping bottom. The nodules on the base of the Drennan design aid grip and almost claw into the lake bed.

I've prepared the feed bait on the bank by simply covering fishery micro pellets in water, leaving for two minutes, then draining them. I leave these to one side for a while to allow them to absorb the water then add a generous helping of Horlicks powder and Green Swim Stim groundbait. You know when the bait is perfect because you'll be able to squeeze it into a firm ball.

The rods I use for this style of fishing are Shimano 9ft/11ft SpeedMasters – perfect at the shorter length for the 25-yard chuck in front of me today.

Imagine if the water was at its normal level! That slope over there is quite steep and you can only realistically stand a chance of presenting a bait on it with a heavier feeder. It's crucial to fish close to islands and I'm not joking when I say that inches literally can make all the difference. Sometimes you'll only catch by fishing right in the mud where the water meets the bank; the line really can be that fine between catching or not, and goes hand in hand with ensuring your feeder stays where you cast it!

There are fish showing all over the lake – amazing really, given the chilling temperatures we're faced with today. Second cast and the rod is soon assuming its battle curve as a carp takes a liking to the banded 6mm hook bait buried inside the pellet/groundbait/Horlicks combo.

The session rolls on and by casting into virtually the same hole all day I have a carp almost every cast. I'm careful not to move the feeder once

it's in the water and I always feel the line as it sinks before leaving a slack line once the rod is on the rest.

The size 18 Drennan Carp Match barbless sees all of the carp I hook make it to the net! What I will say, though, is that hooklength diameter plays an important role and my preference is for 0.16mm Shimano Antares. This goes against the 'heavy is best' school of thought adopted by many. I think a lighter hooklength gives advantageous presentation.

I decide to wrap up the session having caught an already ridiculous amount of carp for this time of year (testimony to how prolific this water is) and I could have kept catching by repeating the same rhythm.

There's no doubt that 400lb was there to be caught, part of which was testimony to carefully considering the importance of the feeder I was using. This simple tip should help to improve your results.

Alan favours a short 9ft/11ft rod for this style of fishing.

Proof that Alan's tactics make all the difference.

Top rigs for barbel

Barbel are like feeding torpedoes when they are in the mood. Here are four top rigs for big-river sport. Resistance is futile!

The Time-Bomb Rig

The idea behind this rig is that, once in the water, the pace of the flow slowly breaks down the contents of the feeder (pellets and paste-like groundbait). Over time the outer groundbait seal 'dissolves' away, which then releases an amount of pellets that drift down to the hook bait. If a large feeder is used, then a number of pellet layers can be released.

Free-running feeder link and buffer stop

12lb to 15lb main line

Size 10 or 12 specialist hook, baited with a 10mm or 8mm pellet

12in coated-braid hook link

The feeder is loaded with a mixture of feed pellets and sticky groundbait

The Method Lead

This is a great way to fish under the large beds of streamer weed during summer sessions. It is best to use a flat, inside-lead feeder and a short hook link. The tactic is to fish an 8mm or 10mm hair-rigged pellet with the lead wrapped in scalded pellets, which stick like glue when prepared. Once in the water the flow slowly breaks down the feed to create an attractive flavour trail.

12lb to 15lb main line

Short, coated-braid hook link

Hair-rigged 8mm or 10mm pellet on a size 10 or 12 specialist hook

Scalded pellets are wrapped around a 2oz or 3oz inline, flat lead

The Hair-Rigged Pellet Rig

This is a super setup for when the fish are playing hard to get on bigger baits. Fished on a running rig, this is designed to fool the fish into thinking there is no hook bait. Using a smaller than normal hook, create a loopless braid hair using a knotless knot, and superglue four small elliptical pellets to the fibres. Cast out with a small PVA-mesh bag of hook baits, which will explode and disguise the hook. The fish will have no idea!

12lb to 15lb main line

The small PVA-mesh bag means that pellets surround the hook bait once the bag melts

8in to 12in coated-braid hook link

Four elliptical pellets superglued to a hair on a size 12 specialist hook

Free-running 2oz or 3oz gripper-style weight stopped by a soft buffer sleeve

The Maggot-Feeder Rig

With all the modern baits being used to catch specimen barbel, many anglers have forgotten just how good maggots are for the species. The trick is to get them obsessed with the bait, so to that end a large blockend feeder is needed to get plenty of freebies down and out on every cast. In fast-flowing rivers it may be necessary to add extra weight in deeper swims. Once the feeder has emptied it will get the barbel looking for more, and what could be better than a big bunch of grubs on the hook?

Barbel love fresh white maggots – and plenty of them!

12lb to 15lb main line

A bunch of white maggots, hooked or hair rigged on to a size 12 or 14 hook

6in to 12in coated-braid hook link

Large 3oz or 4oz free-running blockend feeder

What bream want!

Top East-Anglian specialist Ade Kiddell mixes match, specimen and specialist tactics as he goes in search of summer bream.

Ade Kiddell

Hometown: Norwich, Norfolk
Sponsors: Korum, Sonubaits
Personal-best bream: 13lb 11oz

B ream are seen as the cattle of British waters, as when they get their heads down they will hoover up anything edible that falls in their path. You would think, therefore, that they would be easy to catch, but as Ade Kiddell discovered on a recent trip to Swangey Lakes in Norfolk, it took some trial and error before the bites started coming.

Swangey is a three-lake complex offering East-Anglian anglers a wide choice of species from big carp to specimen bream, tench and pike. There are massive shoals of bream in the venue's main lake that weigh well into double figures, with the average-size slab at around 5lb. These fish were Ade's target for the day and having fished the venue regularly he was confident of a good catch for the cameras.

Feed Options

Spodding is seen by many anglers as something that's done by specimen carp anglers. This might have been the case once, but it's a skill that match and specialist anglers have taken on board to help them gain an edge. It's a quick way to get a large amount of bait out to a mark and you don't necessarily need heavy specialist gear to do it if you don't intend to cast too far – 30 to 40 yards, for example.

Ade used a 1.5lb test curve 12ft specialist rod with a reel loaded with 10lb line. A medium-sized spod was used – his came free with his Sonubaits Spod Mix – and in less than 20 minutes he had primed both his feed lines.

For the session Ade had planned a two-pronged attack – pellets to his right and naturals in the shape of corn or worms to his left. Bream love these, so he wanted to maximise his chances of catching. If the fish then preferred a particular bait, Ade could change tack and fish the same bait on both rods.

Ade would be fishing corn or worm to his left, so to kick-start that mark he spodded out a pint of dead maggots (he chose dead maggots because they won't bury themselves into the lake bed), plus some casters and corn using a very large cage feeder. Each load was plugged with groundbait to stop the bait escaping during the cast.

On the right-hand line Ade spodded five loads of 4mm pellets, plus some corn and hemp, as insurance.

A switch from double hair-rigged corn to the classic worm-and-maggot cocktail saw Ade Kiddell land bream to 7lb.

Ade's Feeder Rig

Medium Korum open-ended feeder

Locked drilled-bullet back lead

15in 6lb hook link

Size 12 Korum S4 hook

Bream Baits Top Tip

Bream will eat just about any food you can think of, but it pays to take a big selection of hookers and feed, as on occasions they can be fussy about what they want.

Groundbait Recipes

Ade's two-rod attack consisted of a Method-feeder setup and an open-ended feeder helicopter rig, so he required two groundbait mixes for the session.

The Method mix needed to be sticky, so he mixed the following two feeds together – two-thirds Sonubaits Super Carp Method mix to one-third Supercrush F1 mix. The large particles in the Super Carp were riddled off, and before mixing the two ingredients he added a few squirts of F1 liquid to the water.

The open-ended-feeder mix didn't need to be so sticky, so for this Ade used two-thirds Supercrush F1 to one-third Supercrush Green. Again, he added some F1 liquid to the mixing water. Once mixed there was enough for a day on the bank.

Tackle For The Job

A large shoal of bream can quickly clear an area of food, so Ade would need to keep plenty of feed going in during the session. An occasional top-up with the spod would help, but a large feeder would deposit a concentration of food close to his hook bait to lure fish in.

To cope with the weight of the large feeders, Ade used two Korum Precision Multi Feeder rods with the Avon tips fitted. Each rod was paired with a Korum KXi reelsloaded with 8lb Korum line. His hook link was 0.15mm Preston Innovations Power line, but he also had 0.13mm and 0.17mm if a delicate presentation was required, or the big specimens arrived. Initial hook choice was a size 16 Preston PR 36 for his hair-rigged baits.

Bream fishing can be a frustrating affair, as when a feeding shoal arrives there can be so many fish that you can suffer multiple line bites. To help avoid this Ade locked a small, drilled bullet, as a back lead, on his reel line three feet above his feeders.

Hitting The Mark

Having spodded plenty of food over his two lines, Ade wanted his feeders to hit the same spot. To achieve this – having at first clipped up on his spod rod, once he had finished feeding – Ade placed the spod on the bank behind him. Then, having opened the bail arm, he walked along the bank, feeding out the line until he reached the reel's clip.

He then did the same with his two feeder rods. He placed the feeders next to the spod and walked along the bank until he reached the spod rod's reel. He then clipped up both the feeder rods and reeled in. He was now confident that his feeders would land over the feed area.

One important tip when setting the casting distance this way is that once you get back to your peg, cast both feeders out empty so that you hit the clip, and then reel back in. This ensures the line is back on the spool under the correct tension to avoid possible tangles.

Initial Feed

1 Ade prebaited one of his two lines using a spod to feed five loads of 4mm pellets.

2 To prevent the particles escaping he plugged the end with sticky groundbait.

3 As well as dead maggots, the 'naturals' line was spodded with hemp and corn...

4 ... and Ade also fed five feeders full of casters and chopped worms.

Hook Baits

1 Ade's trimmed worm accounted for bream to 7lb.

2 The twin-corn recipe accounted for a single fish…

3 … as did the banded 8mm hooker-pellet offering.

Positive Bites

It can be very easy to miss bites from bream, because as big as they can get, they don't give a ferocious bite like tench and carp. Sometimes they might move the bait a few inches before dropping it. Bream have even been known to pick up a bait and stay put, giving you no clue at your rod tip.

To give maximum bite indication Ade fished his rods on sensitively set bite alarms and swingers. The bite alarm would detect any disturbance of the line and the swingers would indicate a positive take or a drop-back bite if a fish moved towards Ade's bank. The swinger is also important in keeping tension in the line to counter any possible tow in the water. It's also critical that your reel line sinks to avoid surface drift, so Ade sprayed the line on both his reels with a 50/50 mix of water and detergent – this degreases the line.

Slow Start

To start off, Ade fished a banded, hair-rigged 8mm F1 Hook Pellet on his Method-feeder setup using a 6in hook link, and on the helicopter rig two grains of corn hair-rigged using a yellow Korum XL Quickstop. A short hair ensured the bend of the hook rested in the first grain.

After each cast landed Ade reeled in the slack and pulled the rods slowly towards the rests. He explained that this allowed him to gain a little line once the clip had been reached, so if he hooked one of the venue's big bream or carp, it gave him a chance to strip off line and unclip.

Of the two tactics used on the day, Ade's helicopter rig easily outscored the Method feeder.

Gear Guide

1 Ade used the largest model of Preston's flat Method feeders.

2 Medium-sized open-ended feeders also did the job on the day.

3 Preston PR 36 or barbed PR 38 hooks are made for hair rigging.

4 Hook links depended on the size of the target fish.

Sport was slow for the first hour, but the regular short tones from both alarms indicated that fish were in the area. Recasting every 15 minutes, Ade was finally rewarded in the second hour with a 4lb bream on the double-corn feeder rig. This was then followed by a 5lb fish 10 minutes later on the 8mm pellet Method setup.

Radical Rethink

In the next hour Ade continued to get little knocks and drop-backs mainly on the corn – it seemed that the fish were taking more interest in the casters and chopped worms from his open-ended feeder than the corn on the hook. This prompted Ade to remark that it could be the worms that were interesting the fish. A re-jig of the helicopter rig was needed, so he switched to a 15in, 6lb hook link and a size 12 Korum S4 hook. This was baited with a trimmed dendrabaena worm and a single red maggot – the classic bream cocktail!

It was an inspired move, as over the next 90 minutes six bream between 5lb and 7lb fell to the worm hook bait. Ade persevered with the 8mm pellet on the Method rig, but the fish showed no interest in the modern bait. Tradition had won the day. Eventually, the bites stopped coming, as the sun reached its midday peak. It became too bright and the bream disappeared – probably to the shade provided by the island trees – so Ade called a halt to the session.

With a big smile on his face as he posed with the fish for the catch shot, Ade explained that his catch proved something that he strongly believes in – when fishing for bream he will take worms, even if he doesn't always use them on the hook.

Reel Line Top Tip

Your reel line needs to sink quickly to avoid surface drift, so regularly treat it with a 50/50 mix of water and detergent to remove the grease.

These are the best of the bunch, with all of Ade's bigger bream falling to worm.

clubkorum

Remember your first catch?

Think back to your first angling experience and the excitement of landing your first fish… now Club Korum has made it even **easier** to share that feeling.

Introduce a new angler to fishing the easy way with our range of **starter kits**, which provide the tackle needed to get started, along with all the **advice** a new angler needs.

Each kit comes with the **How To Fish DVD** and **booklet**, for the best introduction to **pole**, **float** or **feeder** fishing.

POLE FISHING PACK

FEEDER FISHING PACK

FLOAT FISHING PACK

ALSO AVAILABLE IN LIMITED EDITION PINK*

ALSO AVAILABLE IN LIMITED EDITION PINK*

your **angling journey** starts here

www.**club-korum**.co.uk

*Pole and Float packs only

Hold on tight!

It's a challenge but, as Darren Cox explains, with a powerful pole and a balanced setup it's possible to catch big river specimens from a swim where traditional tactics would fail.

Once a fish is hooked, Darren has to rely on his tensioned elastic stopping it from heading upstream into a submerged jungle of branches and weed!

Most of us these days have plenty of 'commercial' tackle. A lot of anglers, especially the younger generation, have grown up on commercials. All that gear is perfect for plenty of different venues, natural rivers included, and today's session is about demonstrating how easy it is to literally take your carp pole and put it to good use on the wildest of rivers!

And when Total Coarse Fishing tasked me with catching some big chub and, if we are lucky, the odd barbel from a river on the pole there was only one venue that sprang to mind for me.

Offshoot

The 'Back Brook', as it is known, at Hampton Lucy, near Stratford-upon-Avon, is as beautiful a stretch of river as you will find anywhere in the country.

The upper Warwickshire Avon here is wonderful and the Back Brook is an offshoot from the main river. It carries a large amount of well-oxygenated flow round some really winding bends, where the flow is impeded by beds of whip-like rushes, shallow gravel runs and bags of overhanging cover from trees on both sides of the river.

The other main ingredient it has, though, is an abundance of top-quality chub and barbel,

as well as masses of small dace and roach.

But, as in all clear rivers in summer, these are not easy fish to catch. You can often see them in the clear water, which means that they can also see you, so watercraft really comes into play here.

Overhanging Willows

I have settled on a swim today that I have never actually fished before; the main reason being that it is so weedy. It's full of chub and barbel, but they live under the cover of the willow trees, which hang down into the water across the far bank. And if I actually manage to fool some out and on to the hook, I will need

Darren Cox
Hometown: Stratford-upon-Avon
Occupation: UK general manager of Garbolino
Sponsor: Garbolino

The Strong Stuff

01 Darren advises that you fish with a strong commercial pole when tackling rivers for chub and barbel. His choice was the Garbolino G-MAX Power Carp.

02 The rigs need to be made of strong stuff.
Elastic: Garbolino orange Bazookarp
Pole float 1: Garbolino 0.3g DC6T
Pole float 2: Garbolino 0.1g DC6T
Pole float 3: Garbolino 0.3g DC7
Float-rig line: 0.20mm (8lb 11oz) Garbo Line
Float-leger-rig line: 0.23mm (9.7lb) Garbolino Squad
Hooks: Size 12 to 16 Drennan Wide Gape

to get them across loads of streamer weed, which grows from my bank to two-thirds of the way across! The only clear patch is a channel, one and a half metres deep and nine metres out in the main flow.

If I were to tackle this swim with a more traditional rod-and-reel approach I would have to fish much heavier than with the pole – my tactic for today. For example, I would need to fish with a decent-sized float or even a leger weight to get the hook bait to the fish. I would also need a heavier main line and hooklength to actually get the fish out through the snags and vegetation. This is okay when the water is coloured or when you're fishing at night, but not in broad daylight and 25°C

The Right Gear

However, my approach today must be absolutely spot-on; as I said earlier these fish are wise and very wary, so before I try to gain their confidence and hook one I need to be sure my tackle is right.

It is extremely important to have a pole that can withstand the abuse it is likely to get. The Garbolino G-MAX Power Carp is my first choice for power on commercials; it's never let me down and will cope admirably with what I ask of it on rivers.

For it to work properly, though, the elastic needs to be strong enough too. Garbolino orange Bazookarp elastic has all the power I need on commercials, but today I will need to tighten it up even more if it is to work effectively for me. I need to be able to control these fish instantly, as unlike on carp lakes there is no open space for them to swim into. If I'm not in control from the first second then it'll all be over – I will lose the fish and spook the rest of them for a long time.

River Rigs

I have set up three rigs for this session. The first uses a 0.3g DC6T, another commercial carp product and a very robust float pattern. Tried and tested on commercials, this sturdy little float has a carbon stem and thick hollow antenna. The shotting is simple – just a few No8 shot, which can be strung out to fall slowly or bulked nearer the hook to get the bait down quickly.

The second rig is the one I'll use to go right into the lion's den! It's a DC7 shallow carp float, which I'll fish right under the trees if the chub and barbel refuse to come out into open water.

These two rigs are set up so that the bait copies the actions of the loose feed to create as natural looking a hook bait as possible, in order to trick the fish into eating it. I fish them at the pace of the river and I try to coincide the run down at exactly the same time as the loose feed, so that my hook bait falls in among the feed as the fish bolt out from the cover to take a few casters before darting back until the next lot of feed hits the water's surface.

Pole Float-Legering

The third rig is an unusual one, which I learnt about many years ago on the River Wharfe, in Yorkshire. We used to float-leger a lot for barbel, so that we could see exactly where our hook bait was and we could line it up with where the loose feed was hitting the bottom. The rig utilises a 0.1g DC6T and an ¼oz Arlesey bomb 30 centimetres from the hook. This setup is specifically for barbel and is tied up on 0.23mm Garbolino Squad Line, which is very strong.

The two rigs for running

through were on slightly lighter 0.20mm Garbo Line. The hooks are all the same pattern – Drennan Wide Gape in sizes 12 to 16.

All these rigs are balanced to the elastic/pole, which gives me total confidence. These three rigs should cover all areas of my swim. It's then up to me to ensure that I am fishing the right rigs at the right time!

Confidently Feeding

When the rivers are so clear it's extremely important to get the fish swimming around for the bait. Get them confident and actively feeding every time you loose feed and you then have a chance of them taking the hook bait.

This may take a long time and you will have to be patient, especially when you can see the fish you are trying to catch. Sometimes they can drive you mad and it becomes an obsession trying to catch one fish, but you need to be confident that if you maintain the constant feeding then eventually they will succumb to the regular trickle of feed falling through the water.

What is interesting is that once one big fish starts feeding it's not long before there are several fish competing. This is when they suddenly become easier to catch, as they are now all in competition for the food.

Top Bait

For me, the number-one bait combination for big fish in these conditions is casters and hemp, and if you're tackling

Once the fish is beaten, Darren wastes no time in guiding it to the net.

Hook And Feed Baits

1 Hemp and casters are still among the top baits for river chub and barbel.

2 A big pot of particles is fed at regular intervals to pull the specimens in…

3 … and to keep the fish alert, Darren also loose feeds before each run-through.

4 At the start of the session, Darren fished with double caster on the hook.

5 However, a single shell looked more natural as it travelled through the water.

fast-flowing swims you will need plenty of each! It's easy to get through three to four pints of casters and the same of hemp in a session, as you build the swim. You may have to feed for a long time before the fish are confident enough to venture out from the natural cover and into the open water.

Apply The Brakes

When you hook a fish all hell breaks loose. You need to get the fish under control quickly. With chub it's about making sure they don't reach cover, otherwise they will leave the hook in the snag and be gone. Constantly changing the direction you put the pressure on from confuses them, and once you get their heads above the water it's all over.

With barbel it's different – get their first run under control or it's all over! Once you have caught that first big fish, you need to be patient again. It takes time to rebuild their confidence until they are ready to start feeding again.

The Session

The static float/leger rig didn't work on the day and I caught all my fish – five chub and a small barbel – on the other two rigs, running the baits at the pace of the river. On another day the leger rig will be deadly.

By improving your presentation and refining your feeding throughout the session to suit the day, you will catch those wily old chub and barbel. It's never easy in such clear water, and it's a real challenge. To catch the better fish you need to counter the conditions, but it's so worth it to catch such beautiful, naturally stocked wild fish. It's a refreshing change for any true angler who loves the natural beauty of rivers in full bloom in the summer. Try it, and if you are anything like me you will absolutely love it!

Fishery Fact File

The Back Brook, Warwickshire Avon, Hampton Lucy, Warwickshire. Controlled by Stratford-upon-Avon Angling Association. Not available on a day ticket, but annual membership is open to anyone. Permit books are available from all local tackle shops in Warwick and Stratford. For more information call Dave Evason on 01564 793260.

By fishing close to and under the far-bank willows, Darren was able to bag himself five chub and a small barbel.

River – middle reaches

There can be few more appealing places to fish than the middle reaches of a river. We explain where to fish for different species.

Reed Beds
Shoals of perch will hide here, constantly on the lookout for small fish or other food items that come within reach.

Deeper Glides
Any bream in the stretch will head for these areas. Use an open-ended feeder with groundbait, worms and casters.

Runs Over Gravel
Roach will love it here, with a hemp-and-maggot approach often scoring for a good catch of fish to 12oz or so. Try legered breadflake for a bigger fish.

Overhanging Trees
Chub spend much of their time in the shelter afforded by branches overhanging the water from bankside trees.

Undercut Banks
These are magnets for barbel but they can be very difficult to get to with a bait.

Left to its own devices, a river's middle reaches will be an ever-changing blend of fast runs, slow glides, gravels, weedy stretches, bends and undercuts.

All will attract fish and the accomplished angler will know exactly how to target each one to get the most from his day.

There will be a variety of different species present – barbel may well inhabit the weedy areas and undercut banks, with chub close by in the faster runs and under overhanging trees. One or two bream shoals will spend their time in the deeps, while roach will gather together over the gravelly areas to intercept food items as they are swept along in the current.

Many methods will work here, from trotting a waggler or a stick float, to casting a blockend feeder for barbel or a groundbait feeder for bream.

Even pole anglers can enjoy good sport here, for roach on hemp perhaps, while a longer pole with stout tackle will allow tiny floats to be pushed under the branches opposite. Even pike anglers are catered for, with a roving approach with lures usually producing a fish or two.

All in all, a river's middle reaches offer something of interest for most coarse anglers.

The truth about carp rigs

Confused about which rig to use and when, if you want to catch carp? Well, according to Marc Coulson and Jon Bones you only need a couple to succeed…

Marc Coulson In my role as editor of the biggest-selling carp fishing magazine in the UK, as you would expect, I receive dozens of letters every day from readers, each looking for advice on how to fish. One of the most frequently asked questions is about which rig to use. There is never a simple answer, as so many variables dictate which presentation might suit a given lake on a given day. Bottom conditions, depths, size of fish, local rules and your bait are all factors that would play a part in the decision.

In any given year, in Total Carp, we must publish a hundred or more rigs, all of which are of use; this proliferation of different presentations can, however, also serve to confuse. If you are new to carp fishing you could actually end up completely baffled before even wetting a line. So, with this in mind, Jon and I have come up with one rig each, which we would be happy casting out into most lakes. I am not saying that these are the be-all and end-all of carp rigs, but they do give a reference point from which to start.

Before talking about the rigs themselves, there are a couple of important things to mention. Firstly, you will notice that neither of us has chosen a coated hook-link material for our rigs. This is not to suggest that they are not effective, but two things have driven this choice – namely the fact that they tend to be

Marc Coulson
Occupation: Editor, Total Carp magazine. Although addicted to fishing on his syndicate water, Marc still enjoys going out and getting a few winter bites from smaller carp.

Jon Bones
Occupation: Media and marketing manager, Solar Tackle. Jon is a specimen carp angler and spends most of his time fishing big, windswept gravel pits in search of whackers, but he too changes tack in winter and goes in search of cold-water action.

Take-Anywhere Braid Rig

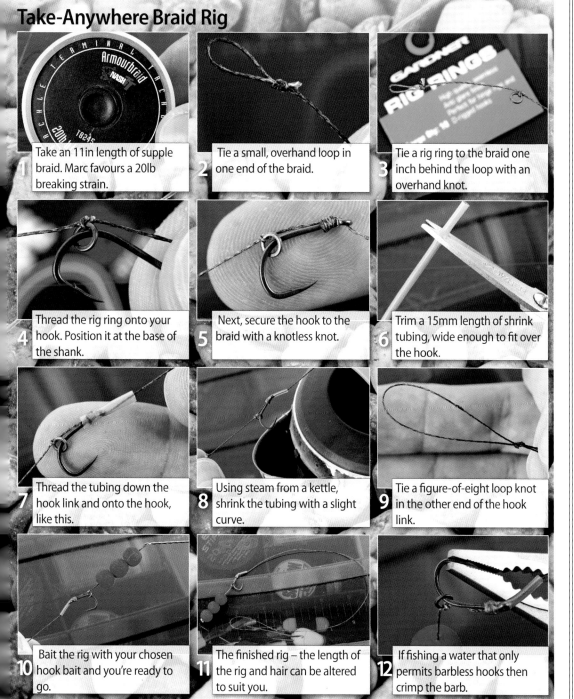

1 Take an 11in length of supple braid. Marc favours a 20lb breaking strain.

2 Tie a small, overhand loop in one end of the braid.

3 Tie a rig ring to the braid one inch behind the loop with an overhand knot.

4 Thread the rig ring onto your hook. Position it at the base of the shank.

5 Next, secure the hook to the braid with a knotless knot.

6 Trim a 15mm length of shrink tubing, wide enough to fit over the hook.

7 Thread the tubing down the hook link and onto the hook, like this.

8 Using steam from a kettle, shrink the tubing with a slight curve.

9 Tie a figure-of-eight loop knot in the other end of the hook link.

10 Bait the rig with your chosen hook bait and you're ready to go.

11 The finished rig – the length of the rig and hair can be altered to suit you.

12 If fishing a water that only permits barbless hooks then crimp the barb.

quite thick, so not particularly subtle, and also that every man and his dog is currently using them. This second point is an important one as so often, just doing something different to those around you can be enough to nick a bite or two.

I accept that coated braids are extremely versatile and, strictly speaking, a good one might be the only hook link you would ever need, but I am using non-coated braid right now simply because I hardly ever see anybody else doing so. Carp, or at least the more pressured carp, learn how to deal with different presentations and the more they see of the same one, the more adept they might become at not falling victim to it.

The take-anywhere braid rig itself is quite simple to construct, but does utilise a sliding ring to aid bait movement and separation, as well as some shrink tubing to safely create a bend in the hook. The choice of hook is driven by the fishery rules. If barbless-only then I will always opt for a pattern with a beaked point, as I truly believe that less fish are lost with such a pattern compared to, say, a straight-point barbless version. I tie my rig off with a large loop at the tag end. This is simply because I always use some form of quick-change swivel at the lead end, making a change of rig simple, especially if I am in a hurry. Finally, it is absolutely vital with any braided rigs – even though the braid I use is inherently stiffer than most – that you feather your cast really positively as it hits the water. This straightens the rig out behind the lead and eliminates tangles.

Jon has long been an advocate of fluorocarbon and he has chosen this as his

This mid-double common is one of many that Jon has caught on fluorocarbon rigs – give them a go.

hook link. I'll let him explain why, but would add that you should definitely consider it. Fluorocarbon is something that I have started to use more and more these days and, if I am fishing a venue where my braid rig is banned (some fisheries don't allow braided

Fluorocarbon D Rig

1 Take a spool of fluorocarbon line, anything from 12lb to 18lb.

2 It is essential that you use a hook with an out-turned eye.

3 Thread the hook onto a length of fluorocarbon, like so.

4 Attach the hook with a knotless knot, creating a 4cm-long hair.

5 Next, thread a circular rig ring on to the hair.

6 Pass the hair through the back of the eye to form a 'D' and then…

7 … pull the hair to make the 'D' smaller and trim off the excess line.

8 Carefully blob the tag end with a lighter to trap the 'D' in place.

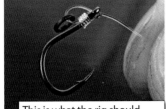

9 This is what the rig should look like. Note the size of the 'D'.

10 If fishing on a barbless-hooks-only water crimp the barb with pliers.

11 Attach a swivel to the other end of the hook link via a loop.

12 The finished rig is ideal for use with bottom or balanced baits.

hook links) then fluorocarbon would be my first-choice reserve.

Jon Bones As Marc mentioned, I've been a fan of fluorocarbon for many years, for both hook links and leaders, primarily because it all but disappears when submerged. With carp, especially those in day-ticket venues, receiving increasing angling pressure over the years, the more subtle you can make your presentation the further you tip the scales in your favour – and it doesn't get much more subtle than a rig that's practically invisible underwater. Furthermore, no matter what venue you target fluorocarbon will be allowed, because nowhere bans its use.

Fluorocarbon is inherently stiff, or at best semi-stiff. While stiff rigs are an advantage in certain situations, this is an exception rather than a rule. I therefore look to build as much flexibility into my fluorocarbon rigs as possible, with the hair and swivel being the key areas.

I don't like using rigs with a stiff hair. This not only affects the mechanics of the rig but alters how the hook bait behaves on the lake bed. Consequently, this makes it stand out like a sore thumb from the freebies, which can be the difference that buys you an extra bite. The easiest way around this is to attach the hook bait to a rig ring presented on a D rig as it is here on the fluorocarbon D rig. Not only does this build flexibility into the rig, more specifically the hook bait, but also allows the length of the hair to be changed easily to suit various baits without the need for tying a new rig.

The rig is attached to a swivel via a loop, rather than a standard knot. The reason, once again, is to build flexibility into the hook link, which aids the rig's mechanics and enables it to sit better on the lake bed. You could tie the rig directly to a ring swivel for a similar effect, but I still opt to attach the rig via a loop.

A hook with an out-turned eye, one that bends away from the hook point, is a must for any rigs tied with fluorocarbon, and monofilament for that matter, when using a knotless knot. First and foremost this eliminates a pressure point on the hook link created by the hook's eye when the hook link is under pressure. This can lead to the hook link breaking, which is something we obviously want to avoid. Secondly, an out-turned eye sits far better on a stiff or semi-stiff material, which aids the rig's presentation.

Bottom or critically balanced baits are the perfect accompaniment to this setup, which can be used with single hook baits, PVA stringers or PVA-mesh bags as well as most lead setups. It's the rig's versatility and the discreet nature of the fluorocarbon that makes it my choice to take anywhere.

This 27lb mirror was caught on the exact rig Marc explains in this feature.

Top rigs for rivers

When the rivers start to flow, it's time to dust off those top-and-bottom floats and big wagglers. Here are four rigs to try with them...

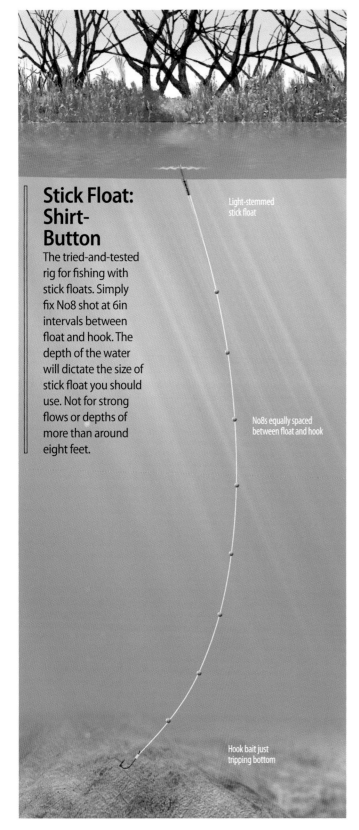

Stick Float: Shirt-Button

The tried-and-tested rig for fishing with stick floats. Simply fix No8 shot at 6in intervals between float and hook. The depth of the water will dictate the size of stick float you should use. Not for strong flows or depths of more than around eight feet.

Light-stemmed stick float

No8s equally spaced between float and hook

Hook bait just tripping bottom

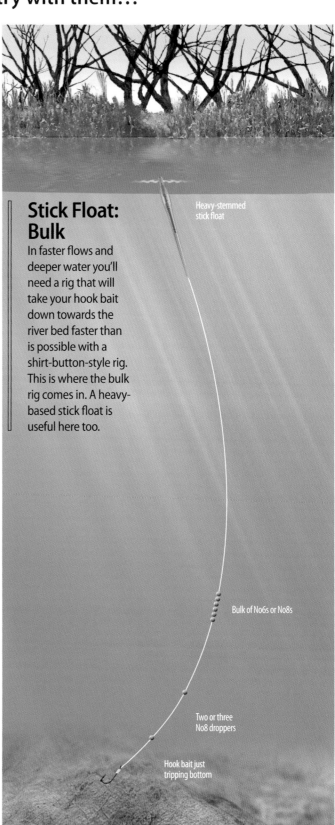

Stick Float: Bulk

In faster flows and deeper water you'll need a rig that will take your hook bait down towards the river bed faster than is possible with a shirt-button-style rig. This is where the bulk rig comes in. A heavy-based stick float is useful here too.

Heavy-stemmed stick float

Bulk of No6s or No8s

Two or three No8 droppers

Hook bait just tripping bottom

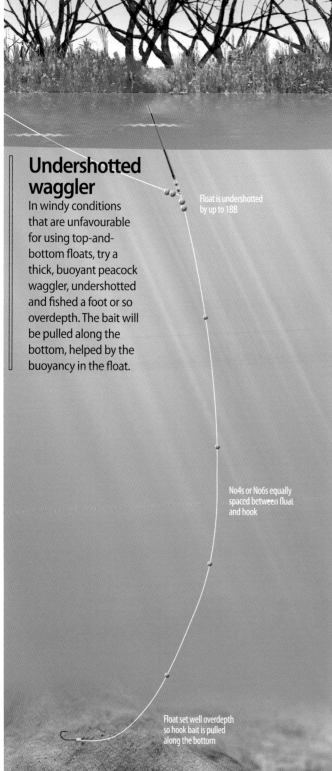

Undershotted waggler

In windy conditions that are unfavourable for using top-and-bottom floats, try a thick, buoyant peacock waggler, undershotted and fished a foot or so overdepth. The bait will be pulled along the bottom, helped by the buoyancy in the float.

Float is undershotted by up to 1BB

No4s or No6s equally spaced between float and hook

Float set well overdepth so hook bait is pulled along the bottom

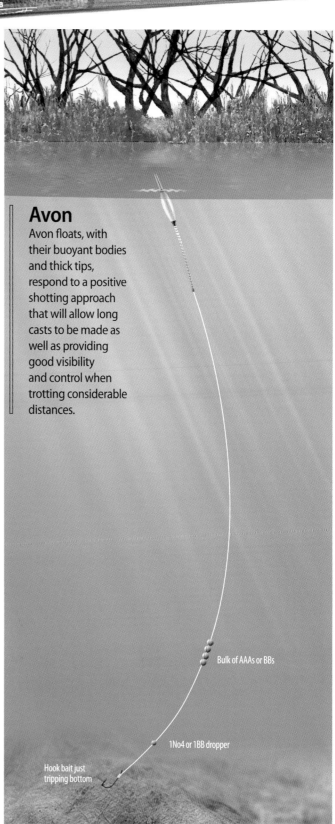

Avon

Avon floats, with their buoyant bodies and thick tips, respond to a positive shotting approach that will allow long casts to be made as well as providing good visibility and control when trotting considerable distances.

Bulk of AAAs or BBs

1No4 or 1BB dropper

Hook bait just tripping bottom

Beyond limits

In winter, when the water goes cold and clear, fish back off into deeper water. Will Raison says go beyond the pole line for silver success.

Whenever you visit any commercial venue you can almost guarantee that most anglers will either be fishing on the pole or with a feeder of some description. However, fish become very docile as the temperature drops, hardly moving during the day, and any food they find tends to be that which drifts past them, or that they find nearby.

They are not always found on the bottom as, depending on the depth of water, they can be found in the layers where the water is warmer. So by concentrating your bait and feed in one spot, bites can be hard to come by. Carp will shoal up and stay in one area for long lengths of time, only feeding during a short 'window' each day. Silver fish, however, will feed for most of the day, because they have to compete for the scraps left by the dominant cyprinids.

To catch these fish, and in most fisheries there are shoals of roach, bream and perch, ex-world champion Will Raison says anglers are missing a trick, especially in the winter months when the water has turned cold and clear – the waggler!

All About Bites

As Will set up for the session on Gold Valley's Bungalow Lake he explained that, when it's cold, it's all about getting bites, and it is no good sitting watching a motionless tip as you could be casting to a barren spot. After a cold night, and given the fact that the water was so clear, the fish would spook with a pole over their heads and a tight bed of feed.

He added that there were two advantages with the waggler: you can overcast and draw the bait back over the feed area without spooking the fish; and with regard to the

Will Raison
Hometown: Ash, Hampshire
Sponsors: Daiwa, Sensas

If bites suddenly stop, don't panic. Wait a while, as a carp might have moved in – it worked for Will!

Will's Waggler Gear

Rod: Daiwa 13ft Airity Match
Main line: Daiwa 3000 TDX
Float: Drennan 2 Swan Insert Peacock waggler
Main line: 3lb Daiwa Sensor
Hook link: 0.12mm Drennan Double Strength
Hook: Size 18 Gamakatsu G-Point Pellet
Other: A selection of shot

Feeding Tip

Feed a pouch of maggots every 10 minutes to create a large spread that won't overfeed the fish.

feed, the bait lands in a spread so, as it falls, it attracts fish from a wide area.

Will also pointed out that he would be fishing beyond the pole line, at around 20 metres, as fish tend to back off a little as the water clears. He reckoned that this is an area that 99 per cent of anglers neglect, with most not even putting a float rod in their holdall.

On The Drop

Having identified that he was likely to catch fish off the bottom, as well as on the deck, Will locked his Drennan 2 Swan Insert Peacock waggler with a bulk of shot. This left the insert still sitting out of the water, so to sink this he added four No8 shot, which he attached at 6in to 8in intervals above his 12in hooklength, which was attached to a small swivel tied to the main line. This swivel acted as a fifth dropper.

Will explained that this on-the-drop setup would target fish in the lower half of the 7ft depth in front of him. He also advised that you should always choose a float that is bigger than you think you need in case the wind increases in strength, which could play havoc with your casting.

Positive Bites

Will's float tip sat a good inch out of the water. He explained that this was because he didn't want too sensitive a rig, ensuring the fish had picked up the bait properly before he was persuaded to strike.

He had also set the rig six to eight inches overdepth to ensure the hook bait settled on the bottom like a loose-fed bait.

Was it also to deal with any tow he might encounter? The answer Will gave was a little surprising, as he explained that any tow would be an advantage because he would cast 'upstream' of the flow and

Will's Tackle Tips

1 To give stress-free casting in the breeze, place the bulk of weight needed around the base of the float.

let the float drift through the feed area. This would allow him to cover a bigger area every cast.

He also added that he wouldn't change the depth at any time, to allow his bait to be slowly dragged along the bottom.

Wide Spread

Because the swirling wind was cold and fairly strong, Will had picked a swim with a high bank behind him, which afforded a degree of comfort. Good advice if you are on a pleasure session and can pick your swim.

Bait for the day was red and white maggots, as Will was looking for a mixed bag of fish, and was after any fish that wanted to feed. He started with double maggots on the hook, to tempt bigger fish. There are some cracking roach and perch in Bungalow.

Before casting he fired out a pouch of 30 to 40 maggots to around 20 metres. It looked a lot of bait, but it landed in a wide spread so, unlike feeding with a pole cup, the feed wasn't all concentrated in one tight area. The theory was that more fish would be covered by the feed, which would draw them in and encourage them to feed.

Will then cast past the feed and wound his float back to the area, where he dipped his rod tip into the water to ensure all the line sank so that the breeze did not drag it and pull the float away from his swim.

2 A small swivel acts as the final dropper shot, and is a tangle-free way to attach the hook link to the main line.

Will picked up plenty of quality roach by fishing with a waggler beyond the pole's maximum 16m distance.

Fishery Fact File

Gold Valley Lakes, Aldershot, Hampshire
Satnav postcode: GU11 2PT
Contact: Office 01252 336333; tackle shop 01252 350963
E-mail: infon@ goldvalleylakes.com
Website: *www. goldvalleylakes.com*

Solid Silvers

Although Will fed a lot of bait, to avoid overfeeding the swim he only fed the free offerings every 10 minutes or so.

As the morning session progressed, he regularly caught quality roach, mostly on the bottom plus a few smaller fish on the drop. The double-maggot offering did cause him to suffer missed bites from small fish. That meant plenty of recasting, but it ensured that his bait was covering plenty of water on a regular basis. It was also noticeable that Will was casting all around the feed area, trying to put the bait right in front of any fish. The tactic saw him catch some quality 2lb-plus perch, roach, rudd, plus a few hybrids.

At one period during the session, the bites slowed and Will suggested that a carp could have moved in. That thought was confirmed a few moments later, when his float disappeared and, as he struck, the fish raced off and his clutch screeched.

The carp was soon tamed, but the intrusion had upset the swim, as bites were non-existent for a while after. Will advised not to panic, and just continued casting and feeding until the fish returned.

The session produced over 20lb of silvers and the carp, all from the 20m mark. Will believed that had he fished the pole or the feeder he would not have caught as many fish, and concluded that if he had to give any advice to an angler looking for a bites, he wouldn't hesitate to recommend the waggler and maggots. He reckoned it was one of the few methods that will guarantee bites, even in the depths of winter!

If you try Will's winter wag-and-mag approach on your local commercial water, you too could end up with a bag of silvers like his 20lb catch.

We've got every angle covered

ET13YISB Buoyant Corn

KD Rig
Moisten and pull hair stop into corn

Side Hooked Corn
Use a small shot to counterbalance the Imitation Corn for small hooks

Tipping a Boilie
Use the long hair stop to lock corn in place when tipping boilie

ET13YIS Sinking Corn

Side Hooked
For float fishing or light link legering with a small hook

Single Grain Lengthways on Hair
Use a short hair stop pulled into the end of the Imitation Corn

Real Grain and Imitation Grain
Use the long hair stop to lock together a grain of real and Imitation Corn

NB: Moisten the hair stops before pulling into the corn

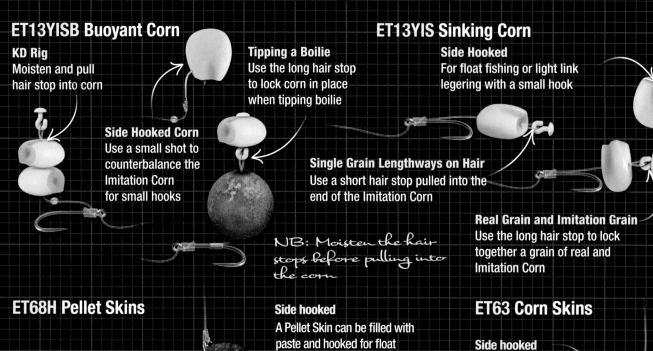

ET68H Pellet Skins

Hair Rigged
Hairstop is concealed inside the skin behind the pellet

Side hooked
A Pellet Skin can be filled with paste and hooked for float fishing

NB: Available in Halibut and Coarse pellet versions

ET63 Corn Skins

Side hooked
Skin's can be loaded with paste or bread

Counterbalance if required

ET49 Snag Safe Run Ring

NB: The Split Ring will release the lead if it should become snagged

Attach your lead via the Split Ring.

Secure the lead on the Split Ring by sliding the silicone tube over the ring and swivel

Pass the reel line through the Adjuster-Stop twice before sliding the two end rubbers on to lock it into position

ET04 Adjuster Stop

To hook

To reel

To adjust hook length, slide off the rubber sections, loosen and slide the Adjuster-Stop to a new position, refit rubbers

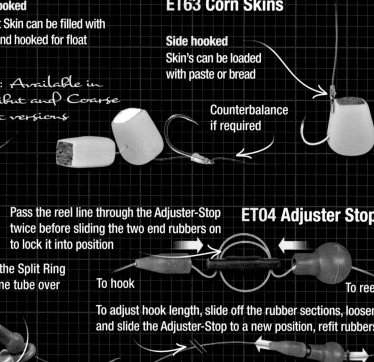

We don't just make Imitation Baits - we also manufacture a range of Terminal Tackle and Accessories to help when fishing for any of the popular species, carp, tench, barbel, chub and more - check them out along with all our other products on our website and see what's available.

Going for gold

After tench, the rudd has to be one of the UK's prettiest fish. They are Gareth Goldson's favourite species, but he pans for his gold on the river.

S pecimen rudd are usually the quarry of specialists who fish the handful of stillwaters in the UK that hold the golden-flanked, crimson-red-finned surface feeders. However, there are some rivers and Fenland drains that are also home to some stunning fish.

One angler who is prepared to travel some distance to seek out 2lb-plus rudd from the rivers is Gareth Goldson, who

Gareth Goldson

Hometown: Cromer, Norfolk
Sponsors: Hardy & Greys, Dynamite Baits
Personal-best rudd: 3lb 1oz

After failing to catch a 'two' early on, Gareth returned to where he started, and was rewarded with this golden-flanked 2lb 2oz River Cam rudd.

Feeling Flaky

1 To fish the flake so that it floats, pinch very little onto the hook.

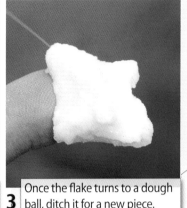

2 For a slow-sinking bait, pinch it on in the more traditional manner.

3 Once the flake turns to a dough ball, ditch it for a new piece.

The early, overcast conditions were ideal as the river was still very clear, even after the many summer downpours.

says that the species is top of his list, and has been for the past few years. And as we walked over the downstream, mechanical, Bottisham lock gate on an almost clear River Cam at Waterbeach, in Cambridgeshire, for an early morning start, he added that, amazingly, the rudd are hardly fished for. One reason he explained was that the fish had to be found, as they live in 'pockets', so there is the need to do some legwork to find them. However, Gareth added that once found, the fish were easy to catch.

Jungle Formula

After a bit of yomping along the bank and over a drain that fed into the river, we arrived at an overgrown area that proved Gareth's point that the venue is little fished. Over on the far bank trees formed a high canopy, and there were odd patches of water cabbages just visible under the surface. A hundred yards downstream, three river boats were moored. These formed ideal cover for all manner of species, but more particularly were one of Gareth's known haunts of specimen rudd. We would visit them later in the session.

Gareth has an impressive record on the Cam when it comes to rudd – in one session last season he bagged eight 2lb-plus fish from another stretch of the river.

Fish Finding

The early morning air was still cool, and there was little breeze on the water. Further downstream, at the boats, there was a good ripple, indicating that there was in fact a headwind – would it impact on Gareth's casting later on?

Being surface and sub-surface feeders, rudd give themselves away fairly easily as they break the surface, feeding on insects and other tasty morsels. Gareth pointed out a few fish feeding downriver and to induce more, and hopefully bigger specimens to feed, he broke up the crust of a fresh loaf of sliced bread and fired it over to the far side.

The first batch saw little interest, but the second offering produced two big swirls, as fish plucked the feed from the surface.

Having established that there were rudd there, and in a feeding mood, those would be the last freebies Gareth would feed!

Crude, But Successful

The tackle required to catch the Cam rudd was very basic. Along with his 13ft float rod and a reel loaded with 4lb line Gareth used a 2.5g loaded crystal waggler and a size 10 Kamasan B983. The float was locked at around two feet above the hook with enough shot to sink it to the shoulder, leaving the fluorescent tip showing. No shot was placed down the line, as Gareth wanted his bait to sink slowly through the upper levels. The whole setup looks crude, but he explained that it's been an extremely successful tactic.

Light And Fluffy

The first few casts were made with crust on the hook, as Gareth wanted to see if he could pick one off the top, but the rudd were a little more cute

than he expected. He switched to a large flake of bread, which he carefully placed on the hook so that it remained 'light and fluffy' to enable the bait to sink slowly through the water.

As the float edged its way downstream Gareth ensured its path stayed true by mending the main line, so that it travelled behind the float.

Quick Bites

The rudd has a slightly protruding lower lip – compared to roach, where the top lip falls slightly over the bottom – so they come up in the water to take food. This enables them to strike quickly. It also means Gareth had to be lightning-quick when he had a bite – not so easy when the bait is 40 yards below him.

The first two positive bites were missed – it's all about reaction time – but on the third pull Gareth struck into a good fish. At 1lb 8oz it was a tiddler compared to the specimens he was used to catching, but still a good start.

Dough Ball

Bites weren't regular – Gareth believed that the small pockets of bigger fish were moving along the cabbage line and often, when he had an indication, it was from a tiny rudd or small chub. After every bite he reeled in, as once the breadflake had taken on water, it turned into a heavy dough ball that the fish ignored. If recast it would sink too fast, so a fresh piece of flake was used on every cast.

Five Top Rudd Venues

1 Frensham Great Pond, Surrey

2 River Cam, Cambridgeshire

3 River Lark, Suffolk

4 Horseshoe Lake, Gloucestershire

5 The Fenland Drains

Gareth's Gear

Rod: Hardy Marksman 13ft Specialist Float

Reel: Fox Match Santos 3200

Main line: 4lb Berkley Float Fish XL

Float: 2.5g and 4g Drennan Loaded Crystal

Hook: Size 10 Kamasan B983

Fishery Fact File

River Cam, Bottisham Lock, Waterbeach, Cambridgeshire

Contact: Daniel Owen on 01223 863825

Controlling club: Waterbeach Angling Club

Website: *www. waterbeachac.co.uk*

Day tickets: Available on the bank from the club bailiff

Gareth also felt that the bigger rudd might have moved closer to the far bank, beyond the marginal weed, waiting for food to drop from the willows and to get away from the brightness of the rising sun.

Move On Down

Three 1lb-plus fish fell to the change in line, but bites quickly dropped off. Gareth moved 40-odd yards downstream, where it was likely that the pocket of fish had also moved. Now out of the trees, the breeze was in Gareth's face, which pushed

against the float on the cast. To counter this he switched to a heavier-weighted float – problem solved!

The Boats

Only one decent rudd came from the swim, so Gareth moved to just above the boats. By casting upstream of them, he was able to present his bait on a line tight to the side of the first boat. This produced two more good-quality fish, but a nest of small chub moved in. It was decided to try the first swim again, as Gareth felt that the bigger rudd were still there.

Big Bar Of Gold

Time was against him now, as the skies were clearing and the temperature was rising. He punched out a bait and allowed it to drift under the willows. Two smaller rudd made a meal of his flake before the bend in his rod on the next strike indicated something much better. Was it a big rudd? Gareth was unsure, but the sight of a big bar of gold reflecting the light as it rose to the surface allayed those fears. The scales confirmed it was a 'two' – weighing in at 2lb 2oz – a fitting finale to an enjoyable session. As the time approached midday, the telltale signs of feeding fish had diminished.

If you can locate the pockets of River Cam rudd, you can reap the rewards!

Lifting the lid on... tench

Ian Welch reveals his 10 best tips for catching everyone's springtime favourite, the tench.

I sometimes wonder how we managed to catch big tench back in the days when there was still a close season enforced on stillwaters. I vividly recall many opening mornings, indeed opening weeks, watching a swim full of activity – float dithering, bobbins bobbing, bubbles popping but nothing actually happening because the tench were spawning, not feeding! Now we know May is the best month to make the most of tench and here are my top tips for making the most of it...

Ian Welch
Hometown: Aldershot, Hampshire
Sponsors: Enterprise Tackle and Innovate Baits

Ian has caught many good tench on a bait positioned at the bottom of the near margin.

1 Search The Slopes

One feature I always look for is a slope, and spending a little time with a marker rod is never time wasted. You should note any humps, bumps, gravel bars or gullies you find, as well as identifying any areas of deep or shallow water.

Although tench will regularly feed on the tops of gravel bars, I have always found the sides and slopes, and indeed the gullies at the bottom, far more productive areas, particularly if they are gravel.

Lakes do, however, vary and it pays to keep your options open to start with. On any new water I tend to fish my first rod on top of the bar, the second on the slope and

the third, if it is permitted, in the gulley. If one rod starts to pick up most of the fish – and one invariably does – I adjust my other rods to fish accordingly.

The biggest slope on any lake is the marginal slope and I have caught a lot of good tench over the years on a bait positioned at the bottom of this just a rod length out. As for depths, tench usually tend to move into the shallower water with the approach of spawning time and drift off into deeper areas as the season progresses, so make sure you know where the shallows dropping off into deeper water are right now!

2 Look For Clues

Tench have a wonderful habit of giving away their location by rolling on the surface at dawn and dusk, with first light, for my money, usually the better of the two. Tench can also be great 'bubblers' and to make the most of your session you should be studying the water closely from very first light, binoculars in hand, and, most importantly, you must be prepared to move in response to what you see.

Tench tend to exhibit two distinct patterns of rolling behaviour. One is a silent 'porpoising' motion. This behaviour usually indicates fish on the move, rather than fish on the feed.

The other rolling is more splashy, caused by tench breaking the surface and using their tail to propel themselves back to the bottom; this is the behaviour you want to see in a swim as it usually means the tench are feeding. Tench bubbles tend to burst to the surface, then fizz and persist for some time with new patches moving as the fish do.

3 Wonderful Weed

There was a time when if you found weed you found tench, but in these days of ever-increasing water enrichment, many natural waters are now choked with weed.

If, however, your venue has patchy weed then the chances are that tench will not be far away. In terms of features we

have already identified gravel slopes as key areas; if your marking reveals a number of gravel slopes and only a couple of them have weed associated with them then that is where you want to have your bait!

Tench are more than happy to feed in weed and by prebaiting it is possible to clear areas large

enough to fish. The traditional method of raking tends to be forgotten these days but it clears a small area for you to fish effectively, colours up the water and puts food items into suspension. The tench are usually in and feeding before you have put the rake down.

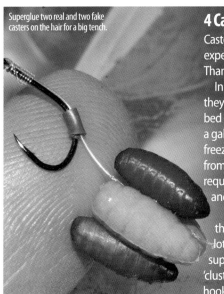

Superglue two real and two fake casters on the hair for a big tench.

4 Casters Are Masters

Casters are the best tench bait in the world, but they are expensive and they are fragile for long-distance casting. Thankfully there are solutions to both.

In respect of cost I have found tench love casters so much they will happily spend time picking them out of a mixed bed of bait, so you only need a couple of pints spread among a gallon or so of feed to make a real difference. They also freeze and a few cheap 'end of week, past their best' bags from your tackle shop can be frozen and used as and when required. They are not as good as a fresh, pale-skinned shell and not great on the hook, but as feed items they are ideal.

As far as their fragility is concerned, the development of the Enterprise Tackle rubber caster changed the rules! A lot of my colleagues only use the rubber version; I tend to superglue two real and two fake casters together in a little 'cluster' to give a beautifully visual and perfectly balanced hook bait.

5 Marvellous Molasses

Tench have a very sweet tooth and it is rare for me to put a tench groundbait or spod mix together without adding a sweetener of some description, and more often than not that is in the form of liquid molasses. Commercially produced as a horse-feed additive, molasses is a naturally sweet, sticky by-product of the sugar-processing industry, packed with vitamins, minerals, enzymes and betaine.

Used neat to glug into groundbait or thinned with water to spray onto, or pump into, pellets, it is the one additive every tench angler should have in their armoury, with a can of condensed milk a very close second!

Sweet flavours, and especially molasses, are a must for tench.

6 Maggot Rigs

After casters the tench bait I would not fish without is red maggots and a bunch of reds is always on my second rod. Despite numerous attempts by various manufacturers to create a maggot clip that works, I have yet to come across a better method than using a fine-wire size 20 hook on the end of the hair.

With maggots threaded over the small hook and up the hair I finish it off by masking the hook point with a rubber grub and squeezing the barb and hook point over so that it is totally blunt. The bait sinks slowly and sits up perfectly, just slightly above the main bed of feed.

Red maggots are second only to casters when it comes to top tench baits.

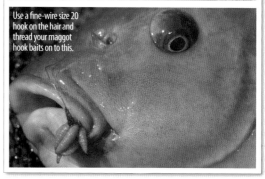

Use a fine-wire size 20 hook on the hair and thread your maggot hook baits on to this.

7 Bits And Pieces

Tench can be very picky feeders, one minute enjoying one particular item, the next going totally off that and absorbed in something different. For this reason I always ensure my tench feed contains a number of small food items, with casters, red maggots, corn, hemp and mini-halibut pellets always present. Other occasional additions include tares, groats, boilie crumb, flaked maize, chopped mussels (the supermarket variety) and chopped worms. A carpet of small items will keep a group of tench active longer than larger feed items and allows for bait changes if one suddenly 'switches off', as they often do with tench (casters being the possible exception).

Enhance your imitation corn by soaking in a sweet flavouring.

Make sure your tench feed contains a variety of small items.

8 Flavours

Enhancing your hook bait with additional flavour to make it stand out from the rest of the feed is a well-established practice for many species and for my tench fishing that means soaking grains of artificial corn or imitation maggots in a tub of neat flavour – or indeed using one of the pre-soaked Enterprise Tackle grains or grubs. Artificial baits, unlike the real thing, retain their flavour almost indefinitely and even after a night fishing in smelly silt your corn will still come out smelling sweetly!

The sweet tooth of tench means the super-sweet flavours are the ones to go for with maple, tutti frutti, ester strawberry, candy sweetener and scopex all excellent.

9 Short Feeder Rigs

When it comes to rig avoidance, tench are well ahead of carp and consistent, effective hooking requires a certain degree of subtlety of presentation, combined with a little rig mechanics – and a very sharp hook.

A maggot or cage feeder fished helicopter-style with a short hooklength (and by short I mean two or three inches!) above it is the most effective way to nail tench over a bed of small feed items – and fishing over such a bed of feed is by far the most effective way to catch tench.

In this situation a long hooklength is a liability, leading to twitchy bites and dropped hook baits because the fish is not having to move far enough between picking up food items to straighten the hooklength and prick itself; a short hooklength gives the perfect bolt effect and ensures a positive indication to strike at.

Use a helicopter rig and a short hooklength to nail a bait over a bed of feed.

Simple maggots in a blockend will often produce a tench or two.

Watching a float is still a great way of catching a big tench...

10 Float And Flake

Watching a crimson tip alongside a patch of lilies may be straight out of Mr Crabtree but for all of my hi-tech feeder rigs and bait flavourings I find there is still a place for a lump of breadflake under a float.

Float fishing gives a sensitivity of presentation and indication that no leger or feeder can match and it allows perfect presentation over those marginal slopes or to that bubbler which suddenly appears in your swim.

The traditional lift method, with the float set overdepth and cocked by a large telltale shot, is still as effective as it ever was and no tench angler should be without the means to fish it.

Corn, worms, maggots and mussels all work well but for me there is something special about a big lump of flake over a bed of liquidised bread or mash (with a squirt of liquid molasses to sweeten it!).

A lightweight pair of chest waders allows Paul Elt to reach places most anglers would think unfishable.

Fish the unfishable

A low and weed-filled river doesn't mean you should head for home. Paul Elt reveals how to get the most from challenging conditions.

Despite the early start the temperature is already climbing steeply as the sun rises towards its zenith and the day is shaping up to be another scorcher. Still partially shaded by the dense far-bank foliage, the tiny River Ivel is a sight to behold. Nestled between modern housing estates and busy roads, the river provides a haven for wildlife that goes unnoticed by all but a few anglers and early morning dog walkers.

The water is clear enough to be bottled and as the intense sun beats down on the surface, every pebble on the riverbed can clearly be seen among the dense strands of water plants. And what plants! In places they completely cover the surface, and in most swims only tiny holes no bigger than a dinner table reveal the polished gravel underneath. This is a river teeming with life, but to the average angler it would appear almost unfishable.

Paul Elt
Hometown: St Neots, Cambs
Occupation: Car transporter driver
Sponsors: Drennan and Dynamite Baits
River bests: Barbel 15lb 14oz; chub 7lb; perch 3lb 9oz

As he stands on the road bridge surveying the scene, top Midlands specimen angler Paul Elt is quietly confident despite the conditions. A regular on this his local river, Paul has devised a highly mobile approach to tackling small rivers that maximises his chances of success.

Low-Light Predators

Two hundred metres from the car park, Paul stops and dons his lightweight chest waders, an essential part of his small-river kit. A thick mat of sedges and reeds has grown out from the far bank forming an inviting floating raft. The only way to position a bait under the raft is to drop it into a 2ft round gap in the reeds. A normal cast would be almost impossible, but Paul stealthily wades out into midstream and, with the rig wound up to the rod tip, simply drops the bait straight into the gap.

The lobworm bait sinks into the gloom under the raft and Paul lets the SSG shot settle in no more than two feet of water before the current gently tightens the line to his quivertip. Small taps begin almost instantly as chublets and minnows investigate the worm, before the tip jags down hard and Paul strikes. With little room to manoeuvre, the fight is short-lived as heavy side strain brings the culprit, a brilliantly coloured perch, to the surface and into the waiting net.

Another perch soon follows from the same spot. Perch feel particularly comfortable tucked into the semi-dark cover underneath dense rafts of reeds and this is a classic spot in which to find them. The constantly low-light conditions are perfect for these ambush predators to use to their advantage as they lay in wait for minnows and small fry.

After the second perch the bites dry up and, having made three casts, Paul is on the move.

Moving On

Paul keeps his gear to the absolute minimum, allowing him to up sticks and move at will. There are just so many likely looking spots to fish that only a tiny fraction of them could possibly hold fish. This style of fishing is all about covering as much water as possible. Even if fish are at home in the heat of the day most are unlikely to be willing to feed, so it is all about putting hook baits in front of as many fish as possible until one makes a mistake.

Fifteen minutes in each spot is plenty long enough, as most times bites will come almost instantly. Paul doesn't introduce any free offerings. If a fish is at home then he wants the first bait it picks up to be the one with a hook in it. This means using baits that will work instantly, such as soft pastes, which will dissolve rapidly, leaking a heady scent trail and naturals, such as lobworms and slugs, which are just too good to resist.

Keep It Simple
Use either a freelined bait or, if you need to cast further, a simple link-leger setup.

How To Make Paul's Paste-Wrap Hook Bait

1 Put a 15mm boilie onto a fine baiting needle.

2 Hair rig the boilie with a 5mm gap between the bait and the bend of the hook.

3 Trim the sides of the boilie to make it barrel shaped – it's easier to attach the paste to.

4 Flatten a small piece of paste and place the boilie in the centre of it.

5 Wrap the paste around the boilie and the hook so that the hook point is just exposed.

The first fish of the day is a bristling perch, which falls to a freelined lobworm.

Clear-river perch are among the most beautiful of Britain's coarse fish.

Paul's Bait

Chub Heaven

With it rapidly turning into a blisteringly hot day, Paul moves upstream searching with his polarising sunglasses for signs of fish. Chub are generally relatively easy to spot. In the warm water they can often be easily spotted in mid-water on the edge of the flow and he spots a few small fish freewheeling in the current.

Barbel are much more difficult to spot as they are supremely camouflaged against the gravel riverbed. Often the only giveaway will be a flash of gold as a barbel rolls on the riverbed, or the sight of the huge coral-coloured pectoral fins. Even when you know they are there, barbel can be almost impossible to spot!

Paul eventually spots a small shoal of chub, including a couple of fish that may top 5lb, sitting on the edge of the shadow of an overhanging tree. Knowing that the chub will spook and not return the instant they think something is wrong, he cannot risk the chance of a small fish intercepting a natural hook bait, so he swaps to a chopped-down hair-rigged boilie wrapped in soft paste.

If he can get the bait into the water without alerting the chub then there is a good chance of a bite within seconds. Fortunately the trailing fronds of streamer weed are so dense that Paul is able to wade to mid-river without alerting them. Rather than drop the bait in immediately Paul waits for the chub to drift under the overhanging canopy before casting. The chub immediately react to the plop of the bait and investigate, and within seconds Paul is into a good fish.

After a spirited fight a long, lean chub hits the net. In the winter months, when they have had a chance to fatten up, the fish are likely to be knocking on the door of 5lb, but at the moment they are considerably less. Chub are almost unique among coarse fish in that they routinely spawn several times over the course of a summer, explaining why it takes them so long to get back to peak condition.

Chub Hell

A shoal of good chub drifting out and picking up some discarded bait on a large clear gravel patch looks like too good an opportunity to miss, but in such open water the chub are going to be alert to the slightest disturbance, and so it proves. With no weed to cover Paul's movement, the chub are already alert by the time he has positioned himself 15 metres above them and settles down to fish.

With so many fish present there is never a time when

You don't need lots of bait for this style of fishing. A few tubs of highly flavoured paste, a bag of Dynamite Baits Red Fish boilies, and a mixture of pellets are Paul's choices. Both chub and barbel love fishmeal and so pellets are a great summer bait, but on some stretches of river they have become overused. By switching to fishmeal-based pastes and boilies you can keep one step ahead.

A tub of lobworms makes a great standby bait that will catch just about everything that swims and is an essential part of Paul's menu. There are some stunning perch in the Ivel and despite being considered more of an autumn and winter species, Paul will target them with lobs should the chance arise.

the swim is clear, so Paul has to risk casting across to the far bank and slowly letting the current swing the bait in to position on a tight line. Already the fish are aware that something is not quite right and although a good fish comes up and investigates the bait immediately, it refuses to pick it up.

An anxious few minutes follow but it is obvious that the chub are now on edge and despite at first glance looking like this was a dead-cert for a fish, Paul eventually has to admit defeat. It is amazing how quickly chub heaven can change to chub hell!

Bar Of Gold

With the sun now positioned behind him, Paul has perfect conditions for fish spotting. As he retraces his steps back down the stretch he spots a flash of gold in a tiny run no more than 18 inches deep tucked against the far bank. After five minutes a barbel, and a good fish at that, sidles out into full view and comes up into mid-water as if it actually wants to be seen!

Swapping to a more powerful Drennan Specimen Barbel rod and 10lb main line that will give him a fighting chance should he hook a barbel, Paul drops his paste bait at the top of the run. With the barbel visible for much of the next 30 minutes Paul is encouraged to stay put and slowly edges the bait down towards the fish. Today, though, it is not to be and eventually the barbel melts away.

A bullet-headed chub is Paul's consolation prize for a sweltering afternoon spent searching more likely looking spots. While other anglers have remained fishless, Paul's ultra-mobile approach has certainly paid dividends with a fine bag of chub and perch, plus the nerve-jangling experience of watching a barbel so close to his bait. From a river that many would have considered unfishable, it is a fine result.

Health & Safety

Always use your landing-net handle to check the make-up of the riverbed.

Venue File River Ivel

Around eight miles of the fabulous River Ivel in Bedfordshire is available from various clubs affiliated to the Ivel Protection Association. Google Ivel Protection for details.

Paul finishes the scorching day with this fine chub on paste.

Natural lakes

Don't be afraid of huge, natural lakes. Here are some pointers to help you make the most of them…

Tench
Large, clear-water lakes often contain huge tench. These will patrol the marginal slope in twos or threes, where you can catch them with a careful approach using sweetcorn or even small boilies.

Bream
Out in the open water a long way from the bank, bream shoals will slowly graze the bottom looking for food. Patience with feeder tackle will reap the rewards here.

Perch
Any bankside or underwater features will attract these smaller predators. In large lakes, some perch will grow to a good size. Small spinners or worms will be best.

Pike

There'll be big pike in big lakes but locating them will be difficult. Look for shoals of small fish like roach and perch and a pike or two won't be far away.

Roach

Large shoals of roach will spend much of their time within casting distance of the bank. Larger fish will swim in small groups further out.

L arge, natural lakes can be a daunting prospect for anglers fishing them for the first time.

They are often open to the elements, with sometimes clear water and little in the way of visible features.

However, the rewards can be immense for anglers prepared to put a little time and effort into their fishing. The fish in natural lakes are often of a high average size, with vast shoals of bream, roach and perch all offering the potential for a good catch.

This rich food source in such a large expanse of water also means that predators grow large. Pike in excess of 30lb are taken every year in waters like this.

There are several factors that should determine your approach on a lake like this. In winter, fish with the wind behind you; you'll also need to cast a good distance out as the margins of natural lakes are often shallow and slope only gradually out to the main body of water.

Vast expanses of water offer
the chance of great sport when
smaller lakes are frozen. Here Rob
Wootton nets a quality roach from
Northamptonshire's Naseby Reservoir.

Worth getting up for!

Winter weather may do its best to make us stay indoors, but Rob Wootton knows exactly what to do to make himself get out of bed for a day on the bank.

Are you one of those anglers who, on opening the curtains, slips back under the duvet at the first sign of wintry weather? Get over it! Fishing in winter can be a rewarding experience as long as you just remember a few key things.

First, it goes without saying that you need to keep warm. Several layers of thin, thermal clothing, a hat and thermal boots will keep out the chill. Take a flask of hot soup and drink small amounts regularly throughout the day.

Fishing with a friend is wise, while, of course, it helps if you know there's a good chance of catching something. The sight of a float going under or a tip going round does wonders for the circulation!

Which is where we come in. Using our network of Britain's top anglers, we're confident that we can keep you catching all winter long. With years of experience behind them, our anglers know what to do and where to go. None more so than Rob Wootton. Rob has been fishing for most of his 28 years, and can truly be called an all-rounder with many competition wins and specimen fish to his credit. He's even caught a sturgeon from his local canal! If anyone can find the fish, Rob can.

Where To Go

With temperatures plummeting, Rob needs to think carefully about his winter session. The mercury has hardly risen above zero for days and this severely restricts his options. First, many smaller stillwaters are frozen over with several inches of ice making fishing impossible. Second, many species will simply not feed in these conditions. Take carp for instance. Normally so reliable in commercial fisheries, carp become largely dormant once the temperature of the surrounding water dips to 5°C

Rob Wootton
Hometown: Leicester
Sponsors: Shimano and Dynamite Baits
Occupation: Angling consultant

for a day or two. Carp are a warm-water species and aren't native to the British Isles.

However, roach are a different proposition. This hardy species will feed even in the coldest of temperatures, and Rob has decided they are to be his target today. So that only leaves the thorny question of where to go. Rivers are in flood, many lakes are frozen, but larger stillwaters are not. Big expanses of water tend not to freeze as readily as smaller ones, and Naseby Reservoir is a good example. This 93-acre lake in Northamptonshire is controlled by British Waterways and contains lots of carp, pike and even catfish, but it's also home to hordes of roach from a few ounces to well over 1lb and Rob has heard they've been feeding well. That's the venue sorted then!

Swim Selection

Large reservoirs like Naseby can be a daunting prospect to the first-time visitor, even if you know they are fishing well. Rob's advice here is twofold: find out

Rob's Tackle Tips

1 Always mark the depth of your swim on your pole against the top of your float.

2 Scale down your terminal tackle for roach.

3 Forget your thick hollow elastics – solid No4 to 6 is perfect.

the productive areas and, especially in winter, fish in comfort. Discovering the best areas is easy – ask the bailiff or a local tackle dealer, even an angler you know who fishes the lake regularly.

Usually, the roach shoals will be in the deeper water in winter on a reservoir, and that means the dam wall. The beauty of fishing from the dam wall is that there is likely to be deep water close to the bank, so you won't need to fish far out. Rob says that he wants to fish in water that is five feet deep as a minimum.

On arrival at the reservoir, he is pleased to see only a gentle ripple brushing the surface. It's very cold, but only a short walk to the middle of

the dam wall where he starts to set up his gear.

Pole fishing is the obvious choice today and Rob soon attaches what he calls a 'winter rig' to his pole tip. He plumbs the depth and is pleased to find six feet of water around eight metres from the bank. Plumbing a little closer in and further out reveals that the bottom slopes gently away. This is perfect. Too steep a slope and his feed wouldn't stay put. A gentle slope will allow Rob to alter his presentation just by fishing a little further out or closer in with the same rig.

Rob's Rig

The rig features a float that takes 10 No10 shot, with a

Rob's Rig Bits

Main line: 0.12mm
Hooklength: 8in of 0.10mm
Hook: Size 16 strong but fine model
Float: 10 No10 model, with wire stem, pear-shaped body, plastic antenna
Elastic: Solid No4 to No6

Regular Loose Feed

1 Casters will always attract the better-quality roach…

2 …while maggots are introduced early on to attract every size of fish.

Don't be put off by the amount of water in front of you; often the fish will be found within a few metres of the bank.

pear-shaped body, orange plastic antenna and wire stem. Rob likes to use wire-stemmed floats because they settle quickly in the water and are very stable, which is useful on big lakes that can 'tow' a lot.

The rig is shotted with eight No8s down the line, fixed in what Rob calls a 'reverse taper'. The first shot is placed at around mid-depth and the last shot is fixed just above the 8in hooklength. The other six No10s are fixed in between, initially close together but gradually getting further apart as they get closer to the hook. Rob has caught a lot of roach using this type of shotting arrangement.

The final two No10s are fixed immediately next to the float's wire eye. They are part of the float's shotting capacity. Rob does this so that he can move them up the line to the pole tip if he wants to try a heavier bait such as sweetcorn, which would otherwise sink the float. Clever eh?

With a main line of 0.12mm and a hooklength of 0.10mm, Rob has a rig that will be perfect for roach. A size 16 hook finishes it – ideal for

his intended caster hook bait. The hook is described as a 'carp finesse' model. Rob likes these hooks for roach as well because the point is straight. He is convinced that in-turned points don't penetrate well through a caster on the strike, leading to lost fish.

Elastic is a No4 to 6, which is ideal for roach but gives Rob a fighting chance of landing any carp or big perch he might hook.

Bait

All you need here are some casters and maggots – one pint of each is enough. Rob always has a can of ready-prepared hempseed with him but this rarely comes out in winter.

As well as these baits, he has two bags of groundbait – Silver X Roach and Frenzied Hempseed from Dynamite Baits. He mixes these together using 75 per cent Roach to 25 per cent Frenzied Hempseed and adds water until a nice, damp groundbait is produced. Roach love hemp and the Frenzied Hempseed groundbait is not only full of hemp, it's also a very dark feed which will darken

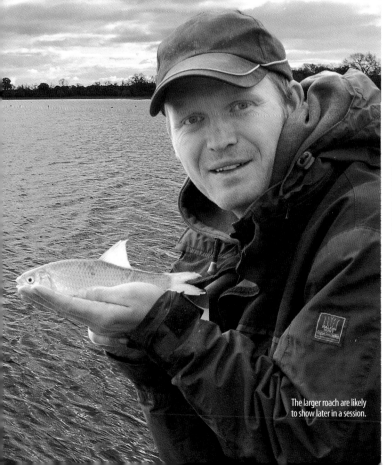

The larger roach are likely to show later in a session.

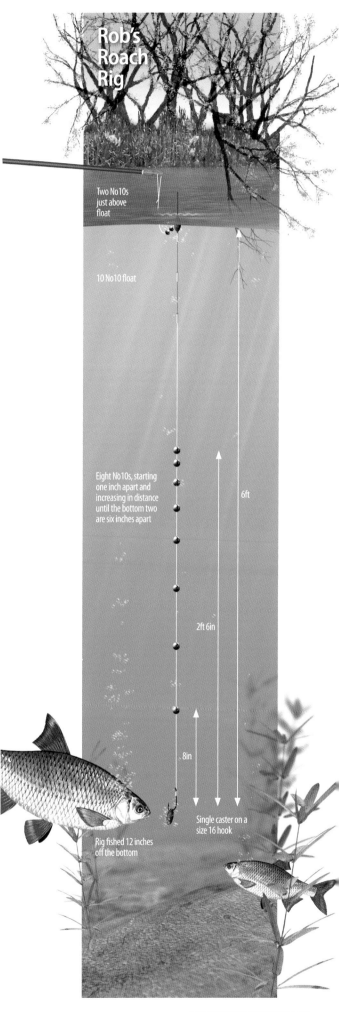

Rob's Roach Rig

Two No10s just above float

10 No10 float

Eight No10s, starting one inch apart and increasing in distance until the bottom two are six inches apart

6ft

2ft 6in

8in

Single caster on a size 16 hook

Rig fished 12 inches off the bottom

the Silver X – ideal in the fairly clear water of Naseby Reservoir.

Feeding And Depth

After plumbing and marking the position of his float against his pole, Rob removes enough line from above the float so that there is around two feet between float and pole tip. He then sets his float so that he's fishing four inches overdepth – a good starting point for winter roach.

Get the feeding right in terms of amounts and regularity and the fish will start to compete. This will result in them losing their natural wariness and they should take a well-presented hook bait without any suspicion. Often this requires shallowing up and Rob fully expects to catch with his hook bait up to 12 inches off the bottom.

The basic premise for feeding is this: feed a few casters and/or maggots very regularly and the fish will come off the bottom; feed more casters and/or maggots less frequently and the fish will stay on or close to the bottom.

However, Rob is at pains to point out that you don't want the roach to come too far off the bottom as they will be very difficult to catch.

The Session

Keen to catch any size of fish at the start of the session, Rob starts off by throwing in four balls of groundbait to which he has added a few casters, then loose feeds a dozen or so maggots every minute or so. He's fishing close enough to allow him to throw his loose feed with an overarm toss.

It doesn't take long before, with a single maggot on the hook, he starts catching small roach of 1oz or so.

Half an hour of this and it's time to change to casters in a bid to catch bigger fish.

Bites slow down instantly, but his first 'proper' bite on a caster sees the best fish so far – a roach of 4oz. Rob now starts shallowing up slightly to see whether the fish have come up off the bed of the reservoir.

At the same time he increases the regularity of his feed, cutting out the maggots completely and feeding casters instead. Soon, the fish are lining up to be caught, with the float disappearing within a few seconds of settling. Even then, Rob is constantly experimenting with the way he presents his caster hook bait, sometimes laying his rig in against the wind, sometimes laying it in in the same direction as the wind. He also lifts his rig out of the water

completely if he hasn't had a bite within 30 seconds or so.

He ends by fishing 12 inches off bottom and keeps the fish there by feeding every 30 seconds. If the fish drift off, he suspects they have come too far up in the water so increases the quantity fed for 10 minutes or so, but less frequently. It all makes for an interesting, enjoyable and warming day.

With a catch of 15lb of prime Naseby roach to show for his efforts after three hours, Rob Wootton is one angler who certainly wouldn't rather have stayed in bed!

Naseby Reservoir Venue file

Location: Carvells Lane, Naseby, Northants
Contact: 01908 302556. Visit *www.fisheries. co.uk/naseby*
Day tickets: £6 from the bailiff on the bank
How to get there: From Junction 1 of the A14, take the A5199 towards Northampton. Just to the south of the A14, take the rod signposted 'No access to A14'. Follow this road, bear left after 400 yards and then turn right across a field to the reservoir car park.

A cracking midwinter roach catch – certainly worth getting out of bed for!

The Right Feed

1 Dynamite Baits Silver X Roach and Frenzied Hempseed mix up easily.

2 Add a handful of casters and throw in four of these at the start to kick-start your session.

Near Margins

You'll often find small perch here that will provide plenty of bites early on in a session.

Centre Boat Channel

While this is unlikely to be the best part of the canal for fishing, an early morning start will sometimes see big perch and roach taken here. Try casters or a piece of lobworm.

Canals

Britain's network of canals offers some fantastic fishing, but do you know what to look for when you arrive at your swim?

Overhanging Branches

Poke a small but beefy pole rig under the branches of an overhanging tree for chub and big perch. Carp will also live here.

Bottom Of Far Slope

This can be the best place to target roach, in the deeper water to the far edge of the boat channel.

Far Slope

This is where any bream will congregate, often moving further out as the day progresses. Pole fish with worms, maggots and pellets for them.

On the face of it, canals are not complicated. These man-made waterways are fairly uniform in depth and contours, broken only by lock gates and the occasional turning bay for boats. They're a far cry from the river we covered earlier. Ironically, it is this very consistency that can make canals daunting prospects for visiting anglers, and one of the reasons why they aren't as popular as they once were.

Canals offer huge opportunities in terms of quality and quantity of fish. Carp over 30lb inhabit some stretches, and there are shoals of big bream and chub on many canals. Roach, skimmers, gudgeon and perch are abundant in most canals. Of course, canals are also loved by boaters, but the good canal angler will actually use this to his advantage, with boats forcing the fish into certain areas of a swim.

Float fishing with a pole or rod-and-line tackle is the best way to tackle canals, which respond to a delicate approach in terms of tackle and bait. For small fish, small baits like pinkies and punched bread are the key, while casters, worms, sweetcorn and even pellets will all catch bream, chub and the occasional carp.

The message is clear: ignore canals at your peril. You might be pleasantly surprised…

◄ Scan the QR code with your phone to find out more about the Elite 88

THE HOTTEST POLE IN THE WORLD - EVER!

ELITE 88 16M PACKAGE
SSP £3250.00

• 4 x *Easy Flow Power Kits • 1 Match Top 3 Kit • 1 Match Top 4 Kit
• Cupping Kit & Cups • Mini Extension • Deluxe Holdall • Clean Caps, DVD

Breathtaking innovation from the world's number 1 pole manufacturer. The remarkable Elite 88 has to be handled to fully appreciate the outstanding balance and rigidity. This is the lightest pole we've ever produced and is further complimented by an outstanding kit package.

*Now supplied with shorter, high performance, easy flow power kits, providing superior rigidity comparable with high level match kits. Every power kit has reinforced power zone wrap for drilling as standard.

Buy now & recieve 1 x Match top 4 kit and
1 x Match top 3 kit worth £400 absolutely free!!

WWW.MAVER.CO.UK

UNIT 8 MERSE ROAD, NORTH MOONS MOAT IND. ESTATE, REDDITCH, WORCS B98 9HL, TEL: 01527 406300, E-MAIL: info@maver.co.uk

Turn to jelly!

Japanese bait giant Marukyu has plenty of innovative products in its range, including a new type of hook-bait pellet – welcome to the wobbly world of JPz!

For any angler who's been on another planet for the past 18 months or so, Marukyu is the world's largest bait manufacturer and its products are now widely available to UK anglers, but when first released the new baits and groundbaits were very different from anything anglers over here had seen before.

Among them, packaged in small glass pots were JPz, best described as soft hook pellets made from what looks like jelly. The Marukyu boffins were confident of the impact they would make in the UK market, and straightaway many anglers used these prototype baits on a few different fisheries and caught well.

Fast-forward to a recent session at the fantastic Glebe Fishery in Leicestershire, where top match angler Andy Kinder was keen to show us the virtues of this unusual bait…

Andy Kinder
Hometown: Sheffield
Occupation: Sales rep for Maver
Sponsors: Maver and Marukyu

What Are JPz?

Marukyu's claims about JPz:

- A 'pellet' that looks and feels like jelly but with totally different characteristics
- No grains means JPz will not split when hooked
- Can be hair-rigged, side-hooked and banded
- Soft texture does not impede the hook
- Will not fall off on the cast because of its in-built durability
- Controlled attractant release, with attractants forming 70 per cent of the bait
- Multi-ingredient formula means the baits are rich and complex
- JPz work in all temperatures
- Can be cut to suit different hook sizes
- The first JPz variety available on tackle-shop shelves was 6mm Ebi, a naturally red jellied pellet made from a multitude of secret ingredients, including high numbers of minute, marine crustaceans. Another flavour and colour is green Nori
- Available in 6mm, 8mm and 10mm sizes

Andy Kinder

A member of the famous Barnsley Blacks match squad, Andy had been among the first anglers to see how these new baits worked.

Having been involved with testing for Marukyu in the UK for several months, Andy was already a fan of its groundbaits and pellets.

He'd quickly taken to the new JPz and had used them to good effect at fisheries like Larford and Barston. Now, he was hair rigging a single JPz and casting a small open-ended feeder to the far side of The Glebe's Pretty Lake.

It didn't take long before the line bites arrived, and seconds later Andy's rod was nearly dragged from the rest by a carp. Several more followed over the next hour, when it was time to try the pole.

Andy had been priming his margins with groundbait, cupping in a combination of loose Marukyu EFG 131 and 120 plus a sprinkling of SFA 441 ground sanagi (silkworm chrysalis) every 10 minutes or so. Loose feeding sweetcorn regularly over the top, Andy gave this swim a good length of time for the fish to arrive.

"Any margin swim will benefit from being fed but not fished," he said. "If I'm in a match with lots of people on the bank I'll often leave the margins alone for at least three hours, but when you're pleasure fishing the fish will usually arrive earlier. Sometimes you'll even see signs as fish boil in their attempt to get to the bait."

For both feeder and pole, Andy used a combination of Marukyu EFG 131 and 120 groundbait, plus a sprinkling of sanagi.

Andy's Feeder Secrets

The far bank might have been only 25 metres or so away, but Andy's feeder casting was very impressive. He shared his thinking on ensuring feeder distance and accuracy in a few simple steps:

1 Cast with a heavy bomb before fishing and once you get the distance right, slip your line behind the clip on the reel spool.

2 If necessary and possible, and if it's allowed, take a walk around to the far bank before fishing and do a little 'gardening' to remove any awkward branches, reeds or other vegetation. Normally you want to be casting as close to the far bank as you can.

3 When you cast, as the feeder approaches the far bank, raise your rod and 'feather' the feeder down so that it lands with a gentle 'plop' and not a 'splash', which might scare fish in shallow water.

4 Raising your rod like this also allows a little extra line around spool before the line hits the clip – useful if a fish charges off after hooking.

5 Make sure you sit on your box in exactly the same way on each cast so that you know the feeder will be sent in the same direction every time.

6 Don't have much of an angle between rod tip and line, and just pick the rod up when a fish takes the bait – you won't need to strike as

JPz On A Band

1 Push a fine baiting needle through a JPz from end to end.

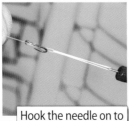

2 Hook the needle on to a micro-band tied into your hook hair.

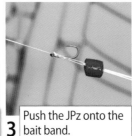

3 Push the JPz onto the bait band.

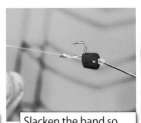

4 Slacken the band so that it expands inside the JPz.

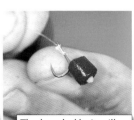

5 The banded bait will withstand the pressure of long casts.

JPz On The Hook

1 A single JPz sits nicely on a size 12…

2 … or you can cut one in half and hook two smaller pieces like this.

carp usually hook themselves against the weight of the feeder.

7 Use a rod whose length is suitable for the casting distance. This might be as little as 9ft for distances up to 20 metres or 13ft for distances over 60 metres.

Margin Alive

Despite no signs of fish having moved into the margins, Andy was fairly confident when he dropped his strong pole rig on to his baited area.

He had hooked a single JPz on a size 12, but commented that a smaller hook would be perfect. A few lifts and drops of the float and it was away. The 3lb mirror carp was slightly smaller than those he had caught on the pole, but he soon had them queuing up.

The key was in the feeding. "What you want to achieve is a few fish feeding confidently on the bottom when your hook bait arrives among them," said Andy.

"I do this by throwing in a ball of groundbait and 20 or so grains of sweetcorn as soon as I hook a fish. By the time I've landed the fish, rebaited and dropped my rig back in again, they're ready for my hook bait!

Try not to feed while your float is in the water. All that will happen is that the fish will come up in the water causing line bites and possibly even foul-hookers – the worst possible scenario."

Another hour in the margins and Andy had done enough. JPz clearly work and they're dead easy to use as well!

Less than three hours' work produced this fine catch for Andy.

Top rigs for roach

Whether you're after a specimen or a great catch of smaller fish, these four rigs will cater for your roach fishing needs.

Helicopter Rig

This rig has accounted for countless big stillwater roach over recent years. It's virtually tangle-free, casts well and ensures your hook bait is close to the bait being released from the feeder.

Avoid snagging by passing a small sleeve over the swivel knot

3in hooklength tied to a swivel locked between two float stops

Use a small, lightweight blockend feeder

Small sleeve is passed over the hooklength swivel

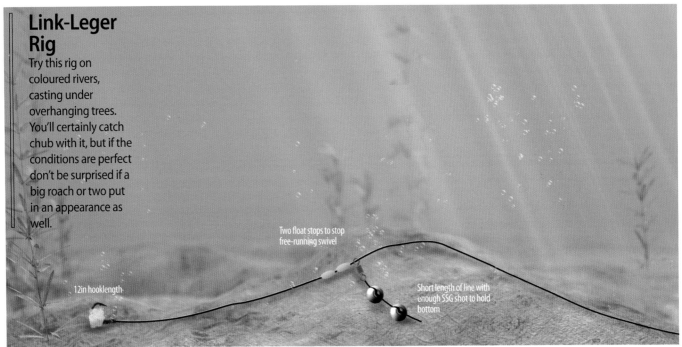

Link-Leger Rig

Try this rig on coloured rivers, casting under overhanging trees. You'll certainly catch chub with it, but if the conditions are perfect don't be surprised if a big roach or two put in an appearance as well.

Two float stops to stop free-running swivel

12in hooklength

Short length of line with enough SSG shot to hold bottom

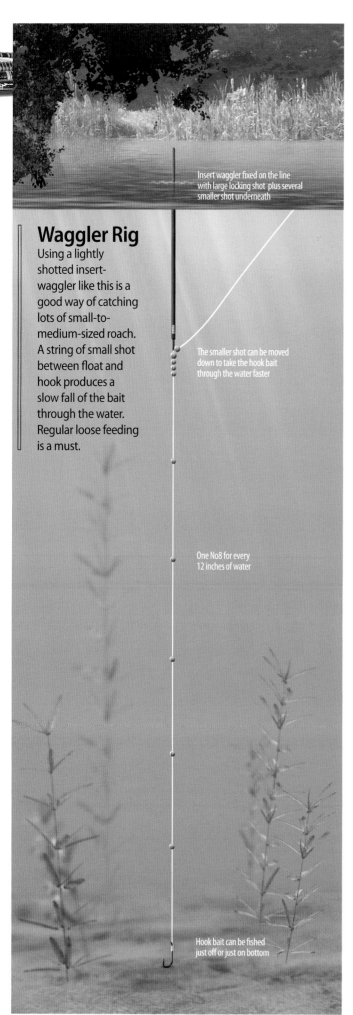

Waggler Rig

Using a lightly shotted insert-waggler like this is a good way of catching lots of small-to-medium-sized roach. A string of small shot between float and hook produces a slow fall of the bait through the water. Regular loose feeding is a must.

Insert waggler fixed on the line with large locking shot plus several smaller shot underneath

The smaller shot can be moved down to take the hook bait through the water faster

One No8 for every 12 inches of water

Hook bait can be fished just off or just on bottom

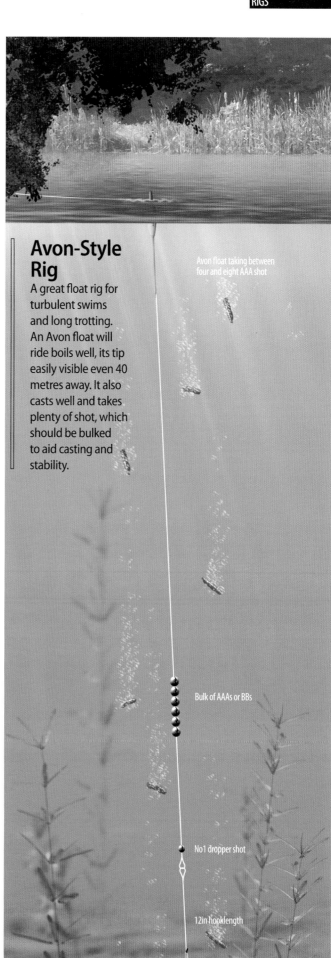

Avon-Style Rig

A great float rig for turbulent swims and long trotting. An Avon float will ride boils well, its tip easily visible even 40 metres away. It also casts well and takes plenty of shot, which should be bulked to aid casting and stability.

Avon float taking between four and eight AAA shot

Bulk of AAAs or BBs

No1 dropper shot

12in hooklength

Fish on! Once hooked, big stillwater chub test your tackle to the limit.

Stalking gravel-pit chub

Mick Brown gets mobile, creeping around the cover of marginal shrubbery in search of patrolling chub in a clear-water gravel pit.

Mick Brown
Hometown: Market Deeping, Lincs
Sponsors: Shimano, Rapala and Dynamite Baits

S talking isn't a tactic that instantly springs to mind nowadays. We do seem to like the comfort of our chairs!

Those who have enjoyed the pleasures of stalking fish will know that setting out to catch a nice fish you have spotted, using all your cunning and stealth, is most rewarding in itself and makes sitting and waiting seem like an old man's sport! Mind you, I'm getting on a bit myself but even so, when the opportunity presents itself to creep up on a fish and catch it, I'll readily take it as it offers the sort of excitement I seek from my fishing.

Over the years I've stalked all sorts of fish, ranging from the obvious species like carp and tench through to species that you wouldn't expect it to be so easy to stalk, like pike and eels. Of them all, though, chub must be among the most difficult, especially in stillwaters.

When an opportunity came up to fish a lake that held a small number of big chub, I took a flyer and

Stalking Essentials

01 The Right Clothing
You don't need to go overboard with camou gear but the clothing should be dull and non-reflective especially if the conditions are bright. Today wasn't a good day to wear my favourite red Dynamite cap, so I opted for a more discreet blue one.

02 Polarising Sunglasses
In circumstances where you are trying to actually spot the fish before making a cast, as was to be the situation for my chub attempt, a good pair of polarising sunglasses is essential to enable you to see through the surface glare. I have caught so many bonus fish simply through getting a quick glimpse of them, which has persuaded me to persevere in the area. On my session, I stood concealed at the water's edge for about 10 minutes and eventually saw the black tails of three or four chub pass by beneath the rippled surface. Time to tackle up!

03 Stealth
Stealth is an essential requirement for stalking and the ability to have the restraint to do everything slowly and quietly while remaining out of the line of vision of the fish you are approaching is vital.

asked Total Coarse Fishing's Steve Martin to accompany me while I tried to catch one for the camera. It was taking a big chance because, in shallow gin-clear water, it was all going to be about just one cast and, if it didn't work out, Steve was going to have to drive straight back to Daventry and have a wasted day! I'll tell you how I got on later but first of all – what are the basics of stalking?

Where To Fish
Firstly, you need somewhere to fish – pretty obvious! Not all venues offer stalking opportunities but you would be surprised what most anglers miss by not being aware and alert. Take the other day, for example. As I arrived at a heavily fished carp water, one of my mates was well bent into a carp that I helped him net. It was a personal best for him at 29lb and he'd just landed it on his tench rod and 6lb line. While everyone else was casting to the horizon, he'd noticed that lily pads to his right were moving every now and again and, regularly scanning the

area, he eventually saw the giveaway tip of a tail showing as a fish upended itself to feed on the bottom of the shallow margin. An hour of careful loose feeding followed and then he made a gentle cast with a float and a hook baited with a single grain of sweetcorn and the rest you know about! There are plenty of opportunities about for those who look for them.

On the estate lake I planned to visit with Steve, a friend had alerted me about some big chub seen patrolling round its gin-clear margins. They sounded well worth fishing for and to gain their interest I gave him a couple of bags of Dynamite Baits 6mm Source pellets to try out on them and check their response. Despite the extremely rich natural food in the lake, they were onto them instantly! Hopefully the pellets would keep them in the area until I arrived.

Stand Well Back

It's essential that you don't undo all your preparation by scaring the fish away with a careless cast. It has to be done in such a manner that will not give you away. This might mean a careful underarm flick or slowly moving the rod into position and dropping the bait, or even casting from some distance away. I chose the latter as the only possibility and would cast while standing about 15 feet from the water's edge, keeping down low.

A Wasted Chance

After taking all the precautions I could and tackling up accordingly, I then had to think about putting the plan into operation. For about half an hour, I tossed small handfuls of the 8mm hard pellets into the swim along with a few soft-hook pellets. It was an act of faith and I had

Having avoided spooking the fish on the first cast, Mick's second chance yielded this super 6lb 10oz chub.

to believe that the chub were mopping them up. I couldn't risk taking a closer look, as I knew it would be so easy to scare them away for the rest of the day.

It was like being a teenager again, sitting and waiting, itching to make the cast, but I knew I couldn't rush it. Finally, during a slight pause in the breeze, I threw out 10 soft pellets and quickly followed with the cast, dropping the float just beyond the free offerings and pulling it back into position, so that the unweighted bait would sink naturally.

They must have been straight on it and the float dipped almost instantly. I missed it, rolled over in the process and ended with the

line in a bush behind me!

Start Again!

Had I blown it? I didn't think so, the strike made little disturbance and I had the presence of mind not to make any disturbance through my annoyance with myself. I let the swim rest for another 20 minutes and rebaited with just one 10mm pellet with the hook point showing this time.

After what seemed an eternity, I made the cast again, baiting with pellets in a similar way. After only 10 seconds or so, the float shot out of sight. I've seen so many floats go under in my time but this felt really special. A beautiful estate lake, rarely fished and I was sitting there in the sunshine fishing for

As she came into sight, her wide body glinted in the sunshine.

On The Hook

1 Three 6mm soft-hooker pellets are a tempting morsel…

2 … but Mick's monsters fell to the larger 10mm baits.

Undershotted
7BB Avon float.

All the shot is
placed under
the float.

FOX
AVON 7BB+

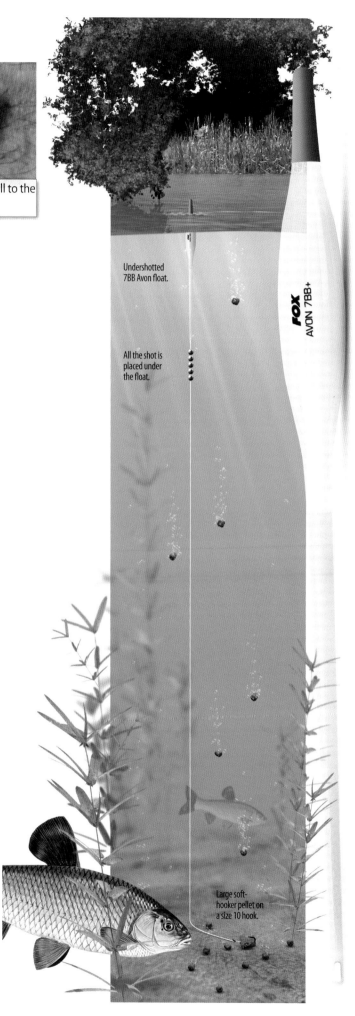

Large soft-
hooker pellet on
a size 10 hook.

some rather special fish.

The water boiled as the confused chub swirled on the surface before heading out to deeper water. Keeping well concealed so as not to affect my chances of another cast if I was to lose this fish, I carefully brought her back. She left the cover of the deeper water and headed for a snag-ridden bush to my right and only severe sidestrain kept her inches from entering it.

When she came into sight, her wide body glinting in the sunshine. Something told me to be very careful; this was a very good fish indeed. As she entered the net, the light hook-hold told me just how lucky I had been to get her back from under the bush and

The Pellet Option

Mick opted for a selection of flavoured soft and hard pellets to attract the monster fish.

The initial feed was hard 8mm Green Swim Stim pellets, which made an attractive splash. Then softer 6mm pellets followed. These sink slower, so are visible longer to patrolling fish.

how important it had been not to panic, but play her firmly.

Steve and I couldn't believe our luck as the scales told us she weighed 6lb 10oz. She was an absolutely pristine chub and as fat as butter, deep-bodied and thick across the back as well. My mission had been accomplished!

... And There's More

The whole feature had been put together in just a couple of hours but, of course, it's not always like that! I had enjoyed the experience so much I really wanted to have another cast but, as expected, the rest of the chub were gone. Time to take another flyer I thought! I suggested that we went pike

fishing for a while and came back in the afternoon. Steve was up for this and so off we went!

They say lightning never strikes in the same place twice, but it was just about to. Approaching the swim in exactly the same way, some four hours later, I got another bite – and missed it! Just like in the morning session, I chanced a second cast after baiting and waiting and – lo and behold – another bite and a fish hooked again! I couldn't believe my luck as I inched another bulky chub over the landing net – this time a bigger one at 6lb 12oz! I've been quite lucky in my time, but a brace of chub for 13lb 6oz is going to take some beating!

" The best of the brace was this 6lb 12oz fish, which is a stillwater best for Mick.

About Mick's Tackle

01 Rod And Reel

Much of the time you just use your everyday tackle that you have for the species in question. When the water is gin clear, though, you do need to ask yourself whether there is anything extra you can do to push the odds in your favour. Mick's rod was a 1lb test-curve model teamed up with a rear-drag 3200-sized reel. A powerful combination, but light enough to enjoy the pleasure of a fighting chub.

02 Line

With the swim quickly dropping away into eight feet of very weedy water, Mick didn't risk losing a fish by fishing undergunned. He was aware that the chub were BIG and this was a very rare opportunity, so he opted for 6lb fluorocarbon. That would be unlikely to break even if a fish weeded itself, but more importantly, its very low-visibility properties would allow the chub to approach with more confidence.

03 Shotting

Mick estimated the depth at about two and a half feet and set his float to three feet. All the shot was under the float, but he undershotted by one BB to make sure he could see it as the breeze was picking up. Mick expected that a bite from a chub would be quite bold and shotting in this way allows the bait to fall naturally through the water.

04 Hooks

Usually Mick would use a size 8 or even size 6 hook for chub, but experience when using small pellets says a size 10 is right for an 8mm soft pellet or a combination of smaller soft pellets. He used Swim Stim Betaine Green soft pellets. The presentation looked just right and the hook would easily pull through without impeding the strike.

05 Floats

To avoid the risk of spooking the chub, Mick chose a clear-bodied float. He was casting into a brisk breeze so went for a 7BB Avon. This is a river-style

float, but he prefers to use them at close range for this sort of fishing, as he can quickly make small adjustments to the depth without moving the shot.

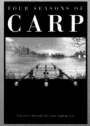
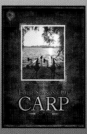

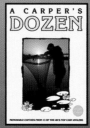

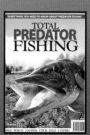

Most of James' bream fell before the boats started in earnest.

Where bream rule the roost

Bream are the fish of the moment on canals these days, and Shakespeare's James Robbins is the man to help you catch them…

James Robbins
Hometown: Kenilworth, Warwickshire
Sponsor: Shakespeare

James Robbins loves getting up early, and as he arrived at the Grand Union Canal at Hatton, in Warwickshire, he had only the dawn chorus for company.

It was 6am, and mist was rising from the glassy surface as he set up opposite the thick vegetation that lines the far bank of Britain's longest man-made waterway.

Fifteen minutes later, a ball of groundbait was dropped gently into the swim, followed quickly by his delicately shotted pole rig.

He didn't have to wait long until the orange tip disappeared and several feet of elastic appeared from his pole tip. The 2lb bream was in the net seconds later and the process was repeated again… and again.

By 11am, work was calling. More than 30lb of bream was carefully returned to the water and half an hour later James was at his office desk in Redditch. Not a bad morning all round!

Welcome to modern-day canal fishing, where bream rule the roost…

Where to fish

Britain's network of canals has changed massively over the past 10 years. Once almost entirely the domain of match anglers, they now hold specimen fish of many species. Carp, chub, eels, perch, zander… most of our canals now offer a realistic target for big-fish anglers looking for a different challenge.

But one species more than any other has thrived during this time. There are very few canals now where you can't catch bream, from skimmers of a few ounces up to proper

£5 a day!

Did you know there are miles and miles of Britain's canals that you can fish for just £5 a day? They're part of the Waterway Wanderers Scheme that owner British Waterways introduced a couple of years ago.

The scheme is designed to allow people to fish canal stretches that are not leased to angling clubs. For details of the stretches available on the scheme visit *www.waterscape.com*. James was fishing the Grand Union at Hatton in Warwickshire, which offers easy parking by the bridge along Dark Lane, which is off the B4439.

'slabs' weighing 4lb and more.

The Grand Union is a prime example. It really is no exaggeration to say that you can fish almost anywhere and stand a good chance of catching bream.

However, in order to stack the odds right in your favour,

James suggested following one simple rule: fish close to features.

"By features, I really mean trees," he explained. "You can be certain that any bream in the area will live where there is shelter provided by them. That's why I chose this swim."

The swim James fished was opposite the middle of a row of trees that provided the perfect sanctuary for bream to keep out of the way of the heavy boat traffic seen on most canals.

"That's another reason for getting up early; in fact, one of

Tackle And Bait

1 Feed one of these after every boat or every couple of fish.

2 Groundbait ingredients – most of it went home with him!

3 Hooks and line.

4 Left to right: Carp dibber, caster float, float with antenna.

5 Best hook bait was caster and pinkie.

Dealing With Boats

Anyone who fishes canals has to deal with boats, and the fact that they stir up the bottom, dispersing your feed all over the place.

The fish don't mind, though; they're used to them. However, it's important to feed after every boat to try to congregate the fish again. A hard ball of groundbait and a sprinkling of hemp and casters should be perfect.

the most important reasons," he joked. "Boaters don't get up as early as anglers so it pays to fish before they start ploughing up and down the canal. They won't upset the fish, but they do upset the anglers!"

Target Areas

Once James had settled into his swim, he explained his plan of attack. Canals are perfect for poles, and that was James' approach.

"It's best not to put all your eggs into one basket and by that I mean I feed several areas of my swim. Looking at the swim, I knew that the main boat channel would be towards the near side because it's where the boats will go to avoid the trees.

"For this reason, I plumbed the depth in front of me to find the slope where the boat channel ended, in nearly three feet of water, and I also plumbed with another section on my pole to find two feet of water. The distance between these two swims was around a metre, which was perfect.

"I also plumbed at angles to my left and right, again in the shallower water. This gave me four target areas, which I could fccd slightly differently to see which the bream preferred. What normally happens is that you catch in the deeper water to start with, before the fish move further across as the boats start up."

Bait And Rigs

You don't need tons of bait for a canal bream session. James had a pint of casters, half a pint of pinkies, a few red maggots, a tin of corn, a tin of hemp, a bag of 4mm pellets and a bag of groundbait… and he took much of that home with him again!

He assembled three rigs:

Rig one: 4x10 caster float, 0.12mm main line, 0.1mm hooklength, No5 elastic, size 20 hook. Shotted with small bulk of No10s. This was the rig for fishing in the shallower water close to the trees.

Rig two: 4x12 float with plastic antenna, 0.12mm main line, 0.1mm hooklength, size 18 hook, soft hollow elastic. Shotted with a strung bulk of No10s. This rig was for the deeper water on the slope at the far side of the boat channel.

Rig three: 4x10 dibber float, 0.16mm line straight through from float to strong size 16 hook, black Hydrolastic. This was the rig for carp, which James would only employ if he saw signs of them.

The Session

After feeding his four swims with a ball of groundbait, plus a few grains of hemp, casters, pellets and sweetcorn, he started with his deeper rig on the far slope of the boat-channel. First fish was a 12oz skimmer, which he caught on a caster-and-pinkie combination, and four more fell in the first hour before he had to change rigs to fish in the shallower water.

After that it was a case of regularly topping up with feed and swapping between his three shallower swims to keep the bream coming for the rest of the session. A great morning's bream fishing in anyone's book!

Many canal swims will produce bream catches like this.

Tench float rigs

Float fishing for tench is one of summer's greatest joys. Here are two great waggler rigs to tempt a big 'tinca'.

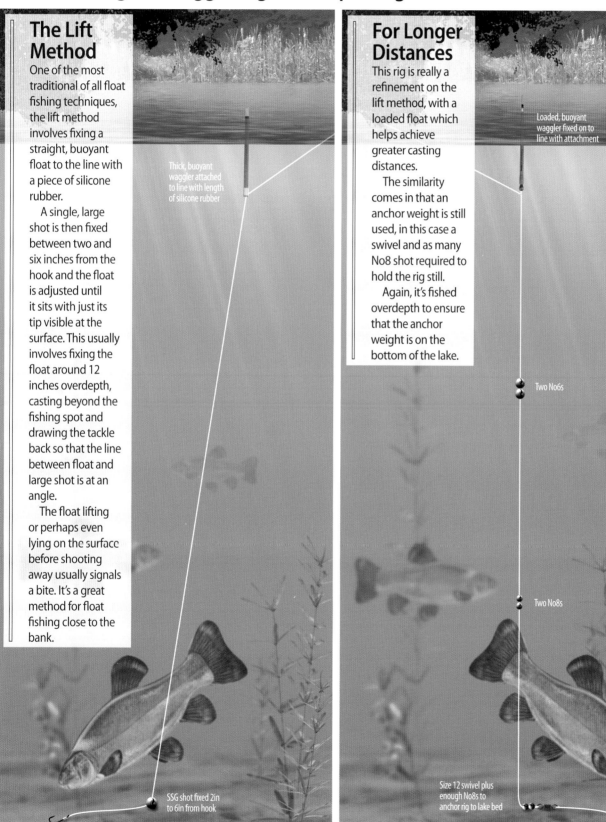

The Lift Method

One of the most traditional of all float fishing techniques, the lift method involves fixing a straight, buoyant float to the line with a piece of silicone rubber.

A single, large shot is then fixed between two and six inches from the hook and the float is adjusted until it sits with just its tip visible at the surface. This usually involves fixing the float around 12 inches overdepth, casting beyond the fishing spot and drawing the tackle back so that the line between float and large shot is at an angle.

The float lifting or perhaps even lying on the surface before shooting away usually signals a bite. It's a great method for float fishing close to the bank.

Thick, buoyant waggler attached to line with length of silicone rubber

SSG shot fixed 2in to 6in from hook

For Longer Distances

This rig is really a refinement on the lift method, with a loaded float which helps achieve greater casting distances.

The similarity comes in that an anchor weight is still used, in this case a swivel and as many No8 shot required to hold the rig still.

Again, it's fished overdepth to ensure that the anchor weight is on the bottom of the lake.

Loaded, buoyant waggler fixed on to line with attachment

Two No6s

Two No8s

Size 12 swivel plus enough No8s to anchor rig to lake bed

Bringing further innovation to fishing.

Simply scan the code to find out more.

Bob's first barbel was lost,
but a change in terminal
tackle soon saw the next
one safely landed.

With many of Britain's rivers running low and clear throughout winter, float anglers need to plan their barbel strategy carefully. Bob Nudd explains how the key to success lies in…

Perfect timing

The tiny orange float tip was barely visible at the surface as it rode the upper reaches of the Warwickshire Avon. Bob Nudd helped its passage by moving his 14ft rod gently against the flow. Seconds later, the float vanished, the rod was swept upstream, and another angry barbel made for the sanctuary of the shallow water below.

The smile on Bob's face spoke volumes. The four-time world champion sees little of this sort of fishing now that he lives in the Cambridgeshire Fens, but after landing his fourth barbel in just three hours, he was seriously considering putting his house on the market!

"This is fantastic!" he enthused as he slipped the five-pounder into his huge keepnet. "Have you noticed how all the barbel have come from more or less the same spot. That's all down to timing, controlling the rig so that it falls at the same time as the loose feed."

A handful of maggots followed, the float was eased back so that the hook bait fell among them, and anticipation mounted.

It's a scenario that is genuinely possible on many rivers up and down the country, but fishing like this isn't for the lazy…

Upper Reaches

The upper reaches of many of Britain's rivers are home to some cracking fish. Chub, barbel, roach and dace can all be found in good numbers, while predator anglers target pike and perch, which can grow to a surprisingly good size.

Winter floods mean that a bomb or feeder approach can often be the best way of catching, but increasingly our rivers are running low and clear, even during those times when they'd traditionally have been running bank-high and raging.

Such were the conditions when Bob arrived at a swim on the Avon. The river, at least 18 inches lower than usual for early winter, was also very clear, with floating leaves and little sign of life.

However, one thing most rivers in their upper reaches do have is flow, and Bob decided where he was going to fish after looking at several swims along the stretch.

"I've chosen this one because the flow is steady and there don't seem to be many boils at the surface," he said. "Boils are an indicator of obstructions underneath. Now these can hold fish, but they can also make the actual fishing process difficult, and fish can sometimes be lost in them."

Looking at the swim from the bank, Bob guessed the depth to be around six feet. He had a consistent run of around 30 metres before the river shallowed massively, indicated by broken water. Swims like this, running down to a ford, hold fish at all times of the year and Bob was convinced that regular loose feed would soon have them within catching range.

Tackle And Bait

Unlike the commercial-water angler, whose bait often takes in a dozen different types, things are much simpler for the river man.

Bob had brought four pints of fresh, bronze maggots, with a handful or reds added. Once on the bank, he riddled off the maize they came in and replaced it with turmeric spice to add even more of an orange colour and also to degrease the maggots, making them sink faster.

The turmeric would also come off the bait to drift downstream in a cloud, much further down than the maggots would travel, the idea being that any fish would follow the trail upstream to find the source.

Bob Nudd
Hometown:
Near March,
Cambridgeshire
Sponsors: Browning,
Van den Eynde

A soft 14ft float rod, fixed-spool reel and reel line of 0.16mm diameter (5lb) provided Bob's balanced setup, while at the business end was a metal-stemmed, domed-top stick float marked 5No6.

"The line is brand new," he said. "New line is best for stick-float work as it tends to be lovely and supple. It also floats better than older line.

"The float has a wire stem, which I like because a wire stem moves through moderate flows like this in a straight line. It also tends to 'ride' any boils or uneven areas of flow better than a thicker wooden stem."

Hook and hooklength choice were tricky. The clear water meant that a fine approach would bring more bites than a heavy one, but Bob was also well aware of the fighting power of barbel.

He finally plumped for a size 18 carbon barbless pattern with a crystal bend and short shank. Deceptively strong, this is a hook that Bob has used with a lot of success for good-sized fish on rivers and drains. A barbless hook does less damage to a maggot than a barbed pattern, and this can make a lot

of difference on a clear river.

However, he was slightly concerned that the 0.10mm (2lb) hooklength would not be strong enough. Time would tell…

The float was shotted with seven No8s to pull it down in the water so that only the very tip was visible. These were spaced equally between float and hook once the depth had been established.

Finding The Depth

Bob didn't bother using a plummet to find the depth. Instead, he set the float at six feet and cast the unbaited rig into the swim. It hadn't travelled far before it pulled under, indicating the hook had caught up on the bottom.

After that, he shallowed up a few inches at a time until the float enjoyed an unhindered passage through the swim.

Bob also stressed that, although he'd found the depth (a tad disappointing at only four feet), he would be regularly moving the float up or down the line by a few inches to provide a different presentation of the hook bait. For example, by increasing the depth, he knew he could slow the tackle down without the hook bait being pulled too far off the bottom.

Three hours, four barbel and one very happy angler.

Bait And Tackle

1 Bait was simple – four pints of bronze maggots with a few reds.

2 Bob started on a size 18 to 2lb line, but soon changed up.

3 Float was a metal-stemmed stick, shotted with seven No8s.

4 Start by feeding this amount. Add more if there are lots of small fish.

5 Single maggot is often the best hook bait as it imitates the feed.

6 Use as fine a line as is safe; the newer the better.

Bob ensured every barbel swam off strongly when returned to the water.

'Killing' Ground

The key to fishing swims like this, Bob explained, is to imitate your loose feed with your hook bait. In other words, he wants his baited hook to be moving through the swim in among the loose feed and behaving in exactly the same way.

The best way to do this is to cast out, feed the swim, and 'ease' your rig back so that it travels downstream at the same rate as the loose feed.

You'll know when you've got it right because you'll start to catch fish, if there are any there in the first place!

There will often be one short area of the swim where everything will be perfect, loose feed and hook bait working in harmony. This 'killing' ground is the place to concentrate your attentions. Make sure your concentration is at its peak here and you'll maximise the potential of the swim.

The Session

When fishing a swim like this, the action is rarely frantic and Bob stressed the need to sit on your box if at all possible. Four or five hours of standing, during which time you might make several hundred casts, is tiring, and Bob made sure

he set his platform up in the shallow margin with his seatbox on top, pointing slightly downstream.

This allowed him to fish in relative comfort, feeding the swim by hand from the bait box on his tray to his left.

He fancied the swim to produce, but when, just 20 minutes into the session, the float disappeared and something very, very large ploughed off downstream, he knew his tackle was undergunned. Sure enough, the fish – certainly a barbel – soon made its escape, prompting Bob to change his hook to a stronger version, although still a size 18, tied to thicker 0.128mm (2lb 12oz) line.

This did the trick, and after a few roach and dace, his first barbel of the day was safely netted. Like the three more he caught during the session, they all fell to a single bronze maggot, and all four came within a short, 6ft area of his swim.

Surprisingly, Bob caught only a dozen or so dace and the same number of roach and perch over the three hours. But he certainly wasn't complaining as he returned them and his quartet of brilliant barbel!

Fish that amaze

Out there are fish that dreams are made of, says John Bailey.

Ian's tench lies on the unhooking mat in the bright light of a brilliantly sunny dawn. It's massive. It lies there framed like a huge, mahogany, timber barge. There's no spawn in it – just a fish with massive shoulders and incredible length. It's an ounce or two shy of 11lb. With spawn you could add 1½lb at least to that weight.

I'm so gobsmacked I can barely take it all in, never mind congratulate its captor. My mind races back to the 1970s when all us young guns were delighted with a 'five', over the moon with a 'six' and desperate for a 'seven'. An 'eight' never crossed the most flamboyant of our horizons. And now this. Whatever will come next in my fishing experience?

It's like the first 2lb roach that I saw, genuinely weighed, again more than 35 years ago. I'd been used to the roach from the north, from the meagre canals, from little industrial pits and ponds where any roach was a good fish and anything over 4oz was a monster. And then I gazed on a 2lb 7oz roach, caught, as it happened, by John Wilson. It looked just too massive to be real. Like he'd modelled it out of plaster

and painted it with brushes. I began to catch them myself; I wanted more and more of them. They intoxicated me. Soon even roach of 2lb 12oz, 2lb 14oz weren't enough. They had to be 'threes'. It was nothing but their simple size that I wanted to gaze on. The wow factor that nothing in life can achieve but fishing.

Like the moment I saw Johnny Jensen's Swedish pike of the mid-1990s lifted from the water. The way it simply stunned us all; its length, its breadth, its depth, its sheer impossibility. It weighed 47lb minimum. The scales weren't built to go higher so we'll never know. All we will remember is a pike that God built to look like a shark.

I'm watching fish in a local mill pool. It's been a day of bright sunlight and the river is running low and clear. I'm seeing loads of chub, some big. There's a barbel or two at the tail of the pool in shallow water feeding on the gravels. Then I see it – a vast ivory shape that swings from the right of the pool across

the current and hides in the darkness to the left. It's a shape so big I can't get my head round it at all. Doesn't it have to be a carp? Can a barbel ever grow so impossibly large? An hour later, the fish shows itself again. There's no mistaking the colour of the fins, the shape of the body, the distinctive way of manipulating the current. This is a barbel and it is over 20lb. If I were never to catch another fish but this ever again I'd be happy.

There are 10lb perch somewhere in the Volga Delta. In the west of Mongolia, there could be grayling of 8lb in weight. I believe in Poland, there are bream to top 20lb with ease. Somewhere in the 'Stans, I'm told, there are carp to rival mahseer. To see any of these! What wouldn't you give to hold a fish that defies logic, imagination and all known natural history?

Oh yes. It's fish that fuel our dreams.

John Bailey
Home: Norfolk
Sponsors: Hardy & Greys
Occupation: Angling guide, writer and tackle consultant